BRANCHING OUT

The story of
PHILIP BOLLOM
and
THE JOHNSON GROUP

JOHN HUDSON

White Tree Books

First published in 1989 by
WHITE TREE BOOKS
an imprint of REDCLIFFE PRESS LTD.,
49 Park Street, Bristol BS1 5NT

ISBN 0 948265 78 7

Typeset and printed by Biddles Ltd., Guildford

Contents

Introduction

The name of Johnson Group Cleaners PLC is not on everyone's lips, but if you live in the United Kingdom there is a one-in-four chance that they were of service to you last time you had a garment dry cleaned. The apparent anonymity lies in the fact that the group is a nationwide amalgamation of large regional companies, nearly all of which have retained their local trading identity while enjoying the benefits of group membership. More familiar in various parts of the country will be the likes of Bollom, Crockatt, Harris, Harton, James Hayes, Kneels, Pullars of Perth, Smiths and Zernys. These are the names, along with a strong Johnsons presence in the North-west, which battle for the company on the high street front in a network of some 750 shops. A textile rental service is also an important part of the business and grows increasingly so, while in recent years the group has conquered new horizons with its imaginative and highly successful expansion into the U.S.A., where it now operates 300 company shops and franchises 170 shops from Florida in the East to California in the West.

In this way the group, stemming largely from family businesses dating from Victorian times or earlier, has grown into the largest dry cleaning organisation in the world. The aim of this book is to trace the steps along the way of this development and to meet some of the men and women, past and present, who have made the Johnson Group what it is today. It is central to the company's philosophy that people matter most, employees and customers alike. This history sets out to reflect this approach, with human interest taking precedent over facts and figures wherever possible.

Its publication marks the retirement in September 1989 of Philip Bollom, Johnson Group chief executive from 1977, chairman since 1985 and a dry cleaning man for more than forty years. It is the story of the company from his angle, leading from his earliest memories of his father's business in Bristol to his increasingly influential role in group affairs. Like the longer history of the dry cleaning industry, Philip Bollom's professional life has been full of rich characters, excitements and disappointments, tragedy and humour; we hope this book will go some way toward capturing some of their flavour, and perhaps give the outsider a taste of an often tough and competitive world that has inspired the loyalty of generations of hard-working men and women.

The author and publishers wish to thank all who have helped with information for this book, most notably past and present Johnson Group directors and staff members too numerous to mention. Many companies within the group have published histories over the years, and several have proved useful sources of information. Special mention must be made of *150 Years*, produced by Johnson Brothers in 1967; *Bollom 1928–1978; The History of J. Pullar and Sons Limited*, compiled by G. H. C. Fisher in 1967; and anniversary histories of the Jas Smith, James Hayes, Crockatt and Harris companies, the latter two written by Ewart Waide Clay. Philip Bollom's commitment to the project and his meticulous preparation of information have been appreciated at all times, as have been the efforts of Mrs. Sheila Sill, his secretary in Bootle.

1 — Bollom — The Early Years

The company in the Johnson Group empire that bears Philip Bollom's family name was founded by his father Ivor – more usually known as Bert – in 1928. Ivor and his brothers Fred and Sam, who were later to join him in the business, were the sons of a baker from Bedminster, south of the River Avon in Bristol, and that was the kind of place where life could be tough if you did not carve out a business niche of your own or opt for a secure job at the great Wills tobacco factories that dominated the view from so many of the tight-knit little backstreets. Ivor Bollom had no doubts whatsoever. He was going to carve out a business niche of his own.

He was born at his parents' recently-acquired home in Whitehouse Lane in 1896; until shortly before then his father John had brought up his family close by in Fraser Street, Windmill Hill. Ivor's early years were blighted by polio, known to that generation as infantile paralysis, and it left him lame for the rest of his life. It was clear that if he was to succeed in business, he would need an organisational flair that would make light of such a disability.

In Bedminster, however, there was no lack of inspiration for a budding young entrepreneur. The term "free market economy" was not one you would hear bandied in Bristol very much in the early years of this century, but the streets around East Street teemed with it, with hundreds of small businesses serving the needs of the community in any number of enterprising ways. Old Bedminster residents still talk of the pavements thronging with shoppers, tramcars clanking along the streets, legendary shops selling cockles from across the Bristol Channel in South Wales, faggots and peas and Sunday joints you could scarcely fit in the oven. Local boxing hopes like Bill Price, Jack Dale and Tiger Pomphrey would show off their talents at the Arcade Hall, there would be queues stretching round the corner for Buster Keaton or Tom Mix at the Stoll and Town Hall cinemas, and boy could meet girl in even more romantic surroundings at Ford Memorial Hall dances. High in the litany of local heroes were a scrawny dog apparently trained to pinch meat from a butcher's on Bedminster Parade and a barber who smashed himself to pieces going over Niagara Falls in a barrel. What gives tales like these added spice to Bedminster old-timers is the fact that the scenes of these childhood memories, the Stoll and the Arcade and the rest, were wiped from the map for ever by the blitzes of the Second World War.

That was the kind of place Bedminster was. It differed from the traditional image of the East End of London in that Bristol, for all its seafaring links, is not and never has been a notably cosmopolitan city, but the cut and thrust of small business enterprise was deep in the fabric of life. Ivor Bollom saw it all, and after his father's death at the age of 40 the realities of making your living became starker than ever, for all his mother's devoted efforts to bring up three sons and a daughter. In 1910, when the time came for him to leave school, he could not wait to get out to work to improve the family finances.

His first job was very much on the other side of the tracks from Bedminster in Park Street, Bristol, the city's steep link with the elegant suburb of Clifton. It was then known as the Bond Street of the West, and the master tailor to whom Ivor was apprenticed was an urbane man who strove to converse with his businessman customers on equal terms, and picked up a great deal of knowledge and *savoir-faire* on the way. After work he would talk to his young apprentice for hours about stocks and shares and commerce in general, about Bristol's merchant venturers of old and of the city's present-day success stories, and Ivor's entrepreneurial fires were further fuelled. By the time he was 21 he was in business on his own.

In his late teens he became a devoted evangelical Christian, inspired by the minister of Philip Street Baptist Chapel. He was never ashamed to proclaim his faith, and for the next 45 years he rarely missed his duties as a lay preacher on Sunday nights. As his commitment and experience increased he went on to become a member of the Congregational Itinerant Society and to sit on the council of Western College and various committees of the London Missionary Society's central board. For a spell he served as president of the Bristol City Mission.

Much of that record of service, however, still lay in the future. In 1921 Ivor married Ruth Gear, the daughter of a departmental manager at Harrods and Baptist lay pastor who shared his Nonconformist commitment, and it was a move that was to have a profound effect on far more than his domestic life. One of his father-in-law's roles at the world-famous department store was to head the dry cleaning section, and he never ceased telling Ivor and his own son

Harold of the business potential there for keen young venturers. Ivor Bollom was reasonably receptive. As the 1920s progressed and the nation's bright hopes of 1918 receded into the hardships of a growing world depression, there seemed good sense in offering to clean people's existing clothes, rather than to make them new ones; in 1924 he and Harold Gear took the plunge.

They opened what they called a Super Valet Service on Redcliffe Hill, still very much in Ivor's home patch of Bedminster, but in spite of the comparatively high prices they were forced to charge in those early days, the venture took off well enough. The two partners were able to withdraw their original capital – £15 each – within a month, and soon began to show a worthwhile profit. Ivor Bollom still thought of himself as a tailor first and foremost, and 15 months later he sold his Super Valet shares to Harold so that he could concentrate on his original craft full-time. But by now, with the General Strike of 1926 dominating the headlines, made-to-measure suits were lower than ever on the nation's list of priorities. In 1927 he felt forced to speculate in dry cleaning once again.

As before, he kept on his tailoring business, but this time he felt far more committed to the cleaning venture. His old partner Harold Gear had died tragically young, so for the new outlet he relied on his own efforts and those of his younger brother Fred, who came in part-time while keeping his job at the tobacco factory. It was with this background that the first Bollom shop opened in 1928, offering the same service as the Super Valet business. A short time later Ivor Bollom was able to add his late partner's two shops to his budding empire.

"Despite my firm intentions of remaining a tailor, fate seemed determined on making me a dry cleaner," he later recalled. "Leastways, with three shops all doing steady business, I appeared to be heading that way, but it must not be imagined that business just flowed in, without effort. My working hours were something like 16 out of each 24. On one occasion, I remember, I even delivered my own handbills from door to door."

Customers of the Super Valet and early Bollom shops would be impressed to see their clothes being pressed by hand, and stains removed with brushes and sponges, a process known as spotting. But such finishing touches were the only ones carried out on the premises; the main business of cleaning was the concern of London contacts of Harold Gear's father, with the clothes buzzing back and forth by train. It meant that a suit would cost 6s. 6d. to clean, take a week to deliver back to the client and be subject to all kinds of risk of loss or damage, and Ivor Bollom was never happy with that. In 1932 he bought an original Burtol 15lb. dry cleaning machine and had it installed in one of his shops at Jamaica Street, Stokes Croft, another busy inner city trading centre in pre-war Bristol. With some 20 shops now to be served, however, it was soon clear that the overworked Burtol needed reinforcements, and the company looked around for a factory as a springboard to future expansion. The answer lay in an old army riding school at Horfield Road, Bristol. It had a floor area of 20,000 square feet, many of them covered in what might euphemistically be described as peat, but Ivor Bollom was quick to see its potential, and bought it without delay in 1935. A year later his plant was working around the clock on a three-shift system.

Ivor and Fred launched a private company, Bollom of Bristol Ltd., on January 1, 1936, its capital of £10,000 divided into £1 shares. Ivor was determined to slash the cost of cleaning and meet the needs of the mass market with mass production, and the Horfield Road factory was a pioneer in putting this principle in action. In 1928 you had to be doing far better than average to earn more than £3 a week, and that did not leave you with many 6s. 6ds. for cleaning suits. By the end of 1936, by doing all the processes on the spot and working virtually non-stop for six days a week, the factory had paved the way for all main lines – suits, coats and dresses – to be cleaned at a new low price of 2s. It also had capacity for dyeing and repairs to help boost profits, and though the shift system had to be abandoned during the war, by then the company had developed enough to absorb the increase in costs.

Centralised cleaning had more subtle benefits. Shops could be more pleasing to the eye – and the nose, for many customers disliked the smell of the cleaning spirits of those times. The branches were not so expensive to fit out, which meant that more could be set up, opening the possibility of one in every suburban high street and several dotted around city centres. Market research has shown that four out of five cleaning customers are more influenced by the geographic convenience of a shop than any other factor. The use of vans led to a speedy service between the shops and factory, and even here mass market principles worked for Ivor Bollom, for reliable motor transport had never cost less than in the 1930s.

In 1937 the company opened 20 new shops, with another 30 in

1938. By 1939 more than 100 branches served an area bounded by Reading in the east, Cardiff in the west, Birmingham to the north and Bournemouth and Plymouth in the south. Turnover in 1937 was £25,000; it doubled in 1938 and by 1939 it was £90,000, the kind of growth that prompted the creation of 10,000 new £1 preference shares to bring the share capital up to £20,000. It was at this time that Fred, who had kept his job at Imperial Tobacco throughout the dramatic growth period of the mid-1930s, at last committed himself full-time to the company, as did two other members of the family, Ivor's elder son David and his brother Sam, two years his senior. Sam worked as a representative for the old-established Bristol soap-makers Christopher Thomas in the days when such salesmen were still happy to be known as commercial travellers, but in an interview shortly before he died in 1980 he recalled that he had been a shareholder in the brothers' company from its earliest days. When he eventually came in full-time he was bristling with sales ideas picked up from a lifetime on the road.

Just before the outbreak of war the company introduced a shoe repair department, a profitable sideline until the 1950s when specialist shops took away trade. As we shall discover later, the Johnson Group would eventually capitalise on this market once again by letting space in a number of its outlets to a shoe repair chain. But all that was far into the future when Ivor Bollom and his brothers surveyed their burgeoning empire in the summer of 1939. In the meantime they had far more pressing matters on their minds.

2 — *Bollom at War*

The first problem posed by the Second World War was one of transport. Bollom was proud of its fleet of modern vans - but the War Office saw a use for them far removed from whisking evening suits and party dresses from Oxford and Cheltenham to Bristol, and though the industry was deemed to be of vital national importance, several vehicles were requisitioned, and the petrol used by the rest was subject to scrupulous rationing. Eleven recently-opened Birmingham shops posed a particular problem, which was solved when they were sold to Quality Cleaners for £1,700. This money was immediately invested in 40 per cent of Quality Cleaners' share capital, so that the company could buy new plant to cope with its increased workload. Such an ingenious little transaction is far removed from the sweeping military and political strategies of the last war, but it perhaps typifies how British business coped with the situation, drawing on all its enterprise and experience to hit upon means of keeping its customers happy and its employees in work, however tough the going.

Sam Bollom prided himself on being an innovator. He inspired an experiment to power some of the company's fleet by gas, but nothing came of it. Later, he was vastly more successful when he used his knowledge of the soap trade to introduce the Newtex process, in which a mixture of resin, wool grease and water deterrent helped to give new body to fabrics left limp by wear. He chuckled to the end of his life about the early days of Newtex, which cost 2s. more than conventional cleaning. The girls in the shops were offered a bonus for selling the new system, but some were left a little baffled by all the science of resin and wool grease.

"But what's the difference between Newtex and ordinary dry cleaning?" asked one client.

"Two shillings," was the swift but indisputable reply.

Petrol shortages and a growing reliance on trains at a time when the major railway stations and lines of southern England were being pounded by Hitler's bombs were not the company's only problem. Bristol was blitzed more severely than all but a handful of British cities. There were times when getting in to work was an act of heroism for some, an utter impossibility for others, and the Horfield Road factory came to a standstill for several days when power and water supplies were shattered. Many companies would have accepted the backlog caused by such disruptions and reminded their customers, in the time-honoured custom of the day, that there was "a war on, you know". That was not good enough for the Bollom brothers. In the short term they contracted out a large quantity of trade to other cleaners, some of whom took advantage of the situation. Ivor was so stung by the prices asked by Quality up in the Midlands that he made a determined bid to acquire a majority holding in them, but nothing came of it and he eventually sold his interest in the company. More constructive was the brothers' long-term contingency plan for if the Horfield Road factory was brought to a permanent standstill. It was decided that subsidiary works must be set up in less dangerous areas, and in 1941 the company bought nine branches and the factory of French Cleaners of Bournemouth for £5,500, and the 26 branches of Caton's of Cardiff, plus its cleaning plant, for a modest £3,500.

These takeovers, apart from being a hedge against the Luftwaffe, had another effect. It seems incredible at a time when people had so many other things on their mind, but business boomed for dry cleaners during wartime – not least because clothes were expected to last so much longer. French Cleaners and Caton's only added to this healthy trading picture, the latter increasing its turnover by a third in a single year, and soon the demands of the Government's Excess Profits Tax seemed to loom as large on the horizon as the Heinkels and doodlebugs. By 1943 turnover had reached a record £123,085, and as the tax was calculated by taking the firm's average profits from 1936 to 1938 and then creaming off all takings above this figure, there were some anxious faces in the Bollom boardroom. The company found itself among those potentially most threatened by the tax; coincidentally, and not as a result of the war, it had grown hugely in the years between 1937 and the early '40s, and now it faced nett profits – compared with a gross profit of 15 per cent – that would devastate its funds for ploughing back into operations.

Ivor Bollom hit upon an ingenious way around the problem. He used the extra money entering the business to pay bonuses to the workers, rather than keeping it as profit. He then issued 10,000 employee shares – £1 shares at 6 per cent cumulative interest – and it need hardly be said that this is the way in which many of the workers spent their bonus money! Eventually all the shares were sold, with the result that the company and its workers did much between them to finance a wartime expansion that saw turnover soar from £25,000 in 1937 to £183,321 in 1945. Profits were at 15 per cent-plus of these figures, and several other small operators had become part of the chain since the 1941 takeovers.

The Johnson Group approach to business philosophy and staff relations will be examined later in the book. For the Bollom company as with others in the group, the war served only to draw it closer to its workers, and to cement a team spirit that lives on in the vastly different social and trading conditions of today. February 1944 saw the publication of the first edition of *The Bollom Letter*, described as "a resumé of the activities of Bollomites at home and in H.M. Forces". Edited at first by Horfield Road works manager Charlie McPherson, it interspersed shop floor gossip and chins-up messages from the management with poems, jokes and news of the lads overseas. We read of Ted Smith, who "instead of heaving trolley-loads of garments about is heaving the main-deck overboard, or whatever sailors do when aboard ship", while several of the boys are reported looking fit and well on visits to the factory during brief spells of leave. But back numbers of the newsletter have their more poignant side, too. That first edition of February 1944 tells of Ken Tregale of the dry cleaning department "with an armoured division up in the North . . . where they play tiddlywinks with manhole covers, and most of them smoke their whiskers after shaving". Four months later the *Letter* is reporting Ken's death in action in France, "one of the younger and more recent of our boys to be called . . . It was as recently as five weeks ago that Ken popped into the works to see us . . . while he and young Arthur Thompson actually met some two weeks later at some southern town, and had a really good night out . . ."

By autumn 1945 the newsletter was reflecting on happier tidings. The August staff outing had been revived, this first one taking the form of a Victory Tour, and no doubt the boys still abroad in Europe, Africa and the Far East read the account of this gentle and cheerful day and wondered whether they would be at home for the 1946 one: "Horfield Road was all agog. Such excitement had not been seen for years, but the Works looked strangely dull and quiet, as if resentful of being deserted. So, too, did Bobby Williams, who was left on guard, apparently the only Bollomite who was not going . . .Everyone was busy climbing into the long row of gay coaches –

11 of them, and 350 people all out to enjoy themselves. The ladies' hats and summer frocks were worth the journey to see – and as to some of the gentlemen's shirts!!"

There was a stop for coffee and shopping at Wells, and after another short run the party reached Cheddar: "Half the coaches at the lower end, and the rest at the upper end of the village. Then the food arrived, and was dispersed from the new black van. Sandwiches in great variety (and quantity) for everyone, cakes, rock cakes, sausage rolls and lashings of tea. What more could one want? Several did want, but not with much success. Someone said it was the 'gorge' of a lifetime." The party inevitably ended up at Weston-super-Mare, where after an afternoon on the pier or round the swimming pool the Bollomites gathered at 5.30 for sports on the green, Mr. Sam being the starter and Mr. Bert (Ivor) the judge. Apart from the usual dashes, sack race and crab race there was a threading needle race for the ladies and a boot race for the gents, and with a first prize of five bob, the stakes were high. Then came more tea, more sandwiches and it was time to go. The first coach arrived home promptly at 8.30, the *Letter* reported, "but several seemed to break down on the way". It seems you had to be discreet about pub stops when you worked for a Nonconformist boss.

The war's last rites were performed at Bristol's Grand Hotel on 27 March, 1947, when hundreds of workers who had served in the Forces sat down to a Welcome Home Dinner of cream of tomato soup or *consommé Julienne*, chicken or turkey with potatoes *au gratin* and runner beans and finally, rhubarb tart and custard or cheese. It sounds utility fare today, but it must have tasted good enough to the men and women who came together there that night, and they gave generous encouragement and applause to Harold Poole's ventriloquist's act, Len May on the xylophone, Robert Cole's rich tenor voice, Ralph Exon with his West Country dialect tales and the violinist Louis Garcia. They toasted the King, stood in silence for fallen comrades, and listened attentively as Mr. Bert and Mr. Sam responded to toasts to the firm and the welfare club. Much was said about the days ahead, too, for within three months the company was to go public in a way that would set the seal on its workers' future security.

Before we leave the wartime years, however, we must note one other development that would have a significant effect on the company. In the summer of 1943 the workforce of Bollom Ltd. was swelled by a further member of the family, Ivor's second son, Philip. At 18 he would go on to serve in the Royal Navy, but that was still a year away, and in the meantime he was determined to find out what it was in dry cleaning that had captivated his father, his uncles and his elder brother. Where better to start than the dyehouse?

3 — The Second Son

Philip Bollom and his twin sister Sheila were born in Stackpool Road, Southville, Bristol on 30 March, 1926, three years after their brother David. The family moved to Long Ashton when the twins were seven, and to another house in the same village when they were twelve, but wherever they were, and in spite of the long hours devoted to business and the church by their father, Philip Bollom looks back on a happy, contented and secure childhood. Long Ashton is only a few minutes' drive to the south-west of Bristol, and closer still to Southville and Bedminster, but even today it keeps a buffer of green fields between itself and the city, while being eminently convenient for all its facilities. If you were a boy growing up in the tight-knit streets of South Bristol you would pass through Long Ashton on your bike or in the chara on your trips to Weston, marvel at this quaint old village so close to home, and swear that if you ever made it in life, this is where you would live. Ivor Bollom had made it, and he delighted in moving his family to this pleasant spot.

From the age of nine to 14 Philip Bollom was a day boy at Bristol Grammar School, after which he was moved to board at Wycliffe College, then in exile at St. David's College, Lampeter, in Mid-Wales. Wycliffe, whose buildings at Stonehouse, near Stroud, were requisitioned by the Government during the war, is a Nonconformist foundation, then boys-only, named after the fierce fourteenth-century reformer who was born in Gloucestershire and earned immortality by ordering the first translation of the Bible into English. "I enjoyed my time there after the first couple of terms," Philip Bollom recalls. "As I came in comparatively late it took me a little time to make friends, but the fact that I was big and good enough to make the first rugby XV helped a little. I was an average scholar, and a reluctant musician in the school orchestra. My father had tremendous zest and enthusiasm for all kinds of interests, and playing the violin was one of them; because he did, then I had to as well.

"The person I remember most at Wycliffe was the headmaster, W. A. Sibly, whose father founded the school. He was dedicated to the moral welfare and spiritual development of each boy, but his

The start of it all for the Bollom family: the Super Valet Service opened by Ivor and his brother-in-law Harold Gear on Redcliffe Hill, Bristol in 1924. Clothes were sent to London for cleaning and the prices, ranging from 2s. 6d. to 8s. 6d., must have raised a few eyebrows in this working-class area.

The first shop to bear the Bollom name, opened in Jamaica Street, Stokes Croft, Bristol in 1928. Parked alongside is Ivor Bollom's Morris Isis, a much-prized early purchase for himself and his family when his business began to take off.

Scenes from the Bollom factory at Horfield Road, Bristol, during the Second World War. Above, in 1939, the work of the young women removing stains in the "spotting" department now took in such tasks as burnishing the braid on naval uniforms, while below, by 1944 the demands of the United States Forces in the West Country were keeping production at full stretch.

Team spirit and a thirst for the great outdoors were popular features of life for city workers in the 1930s, and Bollom staff members were no exception. Above, the soccer team of 1939, many of whose members soon found themselves fighting rather more earnest battles elsewhere. Below, a day in the Mendips for the girls, their Sunday best dresses suggesting that this was a bus outing rather than a strenuous hike.

approach was genial and expansive, and the overall impression he left was one of kindness combined with strict discipline. He was a most remarkable man, but a couple who were friends of his also influenced me in my early years. Mr. and Mrs. Rex Hopes ran the Collegiate School in Bristol, which was the choice for my sister Sheila. At first it was on the Downs north of the city, but later they moved it to Langford Court in Somerset. They must have found it hard going during the school holidays, so they hit upon the idea of opening it up to paying guests. We children went along and had the time of our lives, though even back at home we had two horses to ride in the holidays. Tennis was also a great interest. I played most days at school, and with such constant practice I became a competent player, aided by a 6 feet 2 inches frame that gave me quite a formidable serve. Then there were other things to keep me fit. Broadlands, our second house in Long Ashton, had a four-acre garden, a further ten acres of land, a thousand hens and a few cows. My holiday activities ranged from cutting the grass to milking the cows, with the rate of pay for the job laid down by my father. Your pocket money depended on what you did, and you could say that it was my first encounter with a performance-related incentive scheme.

"I would be the first to admit that, especially in our later childhood, we benefited from all the hard work that my father had put into his business. I do not recall a time when he did not work long hours, and there were days when he carried a load of worry and anxiety. Looking back, I believe hard work alone would not have enabled him to make such rapid progress. He had keen judgement, an astute and shrewd mind, an ability to motivate others and iron determination. A sense of humour also helped, and he enjoyed telling endless tales about his work and the people around him there.

"He was such a tremendous enthusiast for everything. At times mother tried to curb what she considered the more extreme of his pursuits, but she would usually go along with them in the end. There were times when her patience was sorely taxed. For instance, once, without her knowing, he decided to surprise her by buying her a dog. He went to see two, could not decide on which he liked best, so came home with both. Another time he developed a passion for budgies, so we ended up not with a cage in the parlour, like everyone else, but a huge aviary. He was never one to do things by halves!

"My father worked hard and played hard. In spite of his lameness through polio he was a splendid swimmer, and shared our love for a game of tennis. At the age of 40 he took up riding with the Quantock Stag Hounds, no easy recreation for a man who could not grip the saddle with his legs. In later years his keenness for games found expression in his skill at chess and in bowls, a sport in which he represented Gloucestershire. He loved a challenge, and made sure that we children did, too. We were spurred to take him on at games, in argument, anything he saw as a stimulus. It could be exhilarating – and it could be wearing, too! 'Have a go' was his favourite expression, and he made sure we did.

"He was an assertive man who could take a creative idea and make it serve a practical purpose. He could be extremely direct, but he was also considerate, and could convince people by persuasiveness. He was determined and confident, very much goal-oriented, and he was able to enthuse people to strive for those goals. He planned and acted to achieve results with a mind that was always versatile and flexible, and the fact that he could be impatient and irritable when things did not happen fast enough for his liking could not disguise his qualities as a superb motivator. He earned respect and affection from his associates, and inspired the people around him.

"The family always attended church twice on Sunday and at least once during the week. My father was a great 'sermon taster', and had heard most of the great Nonconformist preachers of his day. Names like Campbell Morgan, Joseph Parker, Dinsdale Young and W. G. Benskin were bandied around our house in the way you hear some families discussing Terry Wogan or the stars of EastEnders today, household names in the true sense of the phrase. Dr. Joseph Parker was a particular favourite, perhaps because he was such a colourful character. He was minister of the London City Temple for 35 years, and pulled in huge congregations. My father loved him. He had a favourite story about him climbing into the pulpit and admitting that he did so with some trepidation, since he had received a letter from a gentleman to say that he would be in the congregation that very morning to make a philosophical analysis of the sermon. After a long pause he said: 'I may add that my trepidation is somewhat mitigated by the fact that the gentleman spells philosophical with an F'.

"I have very early memories of being put in the charge of three ladies who worked for my father as seamstresses when he had his tailoring business. I can hardly imagine that I was always welcome around all the needles and threads and patterns, but if their hearts sank when they saw me, they never let it show. A little later I could have been no angel, as I was often taken around by father 'to give your mother a break'. I went to the works with him on Saturdays, and more frequently during the school holidays, and enjoyed helping out in small ways. I don't think it is an exaggeration to say that I had a fund of knowledge about the dry cleaning industry at an early age. Father also took me with him regularly on his preaching engagements. At that age I regarded this as an unavoidable duty, but it gave me a grounding that was to make a strong impact on the rest of my life."

Philip Bollom volunteered for active service on leaving Wycliffe College at 17, but he was not called up until he had worked six or seven months – starting at the bottom in the dyehouse – at Horfield Road during the winter of 1943–44. "In those days people made their clothes last, and dyeing accounted for a significant part of the company's turnover," he recalls.

His service in the Royal Navy lasted from 1944 to 1946, beginning somewhat inauspiciously at Butlin's Holiday Camp in Skegness, on the chilly north-eastern coast. The camp's motto was "Our True Intent Is All For Your Delight", but that was not how the navy seemed to view life, and there was four weeks of unrelieved drill and bull. "I realised then what a sheltered upbringing I'd had," says Philip Bollom. "It was a bit of a shock, but I soon adjusted." After this rigorous month came the best part of a year at radio school on the Isle of Man, a pleasant sojourn followed by brief spells at naval depots in Scotland and at Devonport. Then, at last, came a stint of real travel, at first to Ceylon, where he boarded HMS *Rapid*, and finally, with the war passing into history, an eight-month show-the-flag cruise with HMS *Glasgow*. It was a voyage that would cost the adventurous tourist a not-so-small fortune these days, and while Philip Bollom stresses that not all of it was fun, he admits that a great deal was. As a member of the ship's rugby XV he played against several local teams on travels that took in a three-day wildlife safari in Nairobi, where the climate of a year-round English June came as a wonderful relief after life in the tropics; a less happy stay in hot, dismal, barren Aden; and spells in such exotic spots as Mauritius, Dar-es-Salaam, the Seychelles, Mombasa and Colombo. "It gave me a chance to see something, and broadened my outlook," muses Philip Bollom. "Perhaps national service would still be useful today. It could provide young men with some very useful experience of life."

Such thoughts were not uppermost in his mind, however, as his ship steamed for home in June, 1947. He knew there was the family business waiting for him back there in Bristol, and this time it would make more demands on him than a carefree six months in the dyehouse.

4 — *Post-war Recovery*

The end of the Second World War saw the Bollom business poised for action. The factories it had been provident enough to acquire as insurance against German bombs had both survived, as had its Bristol H.Q. at Horfield Road, and the services of dry cleaners had never been in greater demand. Clothing was on ration, Sunday best for millions of ex-Servicemen was a single demob. suit that was expected to see a good few years' wear, and the concept of the throw-away society was still a generation away. Back in 1946 the spirit of the times was make-do-and-mend. Any service industry that could restore, repair or revive clothes or household goods was on a winner, and the sky was the limit if it also enjoyed the benefit of a bright, forward-thinking management and a willing workforce.

In 1947 came two significant moves for Bollom – its first steps into London, and its spectacularly successful flotation as a public company. The former was achieved through the acquisition of Just Cleaners of Earl's Court, who had nine branches dotted around the capital, including three modern "unit" shops in which processing was done on the premises. Their most prestigious address was in Kensington High Street, where Philip Bollom, fresh from the Royal Navy, spent a happy eight months learning the processing side of the business; this became the first shop in London to bear the Bollom name, in bold Art Deco lettering that helped give the company the cool, clean image it sought. The cleaning unit in the basement handled one-day work from this and other branches and could turn over £1,000's worth of orders a week, but there were still some traditional touches. All other cleaning and dyeing was sent to Horfield Road, and another long-established and now archaic service was stocking repairs, carried out by a girl at a machine on the customers' side of the counter. Nevertheless, the entire package was enough to convince a reporter from *Power Laundry* magazine that Kensington High Street was a glimpse of the future, and inspire a glowing feature headed: "Is This London's Finest Dry Cleaning Depot?"

By this time Bollom had some 180 shops over an ever-widening area, and turnover was touching £200,000 a year. Ivor and his brothers saw that the way ahead was to go public, and in June there was an issue of 940,000 ordinary shares of a shilling; by November they felt able to issue 200,000 more shilling shares, and with 13,000 extra preference shares at £1 each, the firm's capital was raised to £100,000. The year 1949 saw employees' shares changed into preference shares, so that by 1950 the share capital was £40,000 of preference shares and £60,000 of ordinary shilling shares. Through all this Philip Bollom was learning his trade. After Kensington he spent some time in the Bristol works and at a shop in the city, and in 1949, the year he married his first wife Patricia, he was given his earliest significant role in the family firm when he became works manager at Horfield Road.

The early 1950s were boom years for dry cleaning. People were beginning to feel that they had a little more money in their pockets, but by today's standards cash was still tight, and anything left over from the weekly budget for clothes was more likely to be spent on cleaning or dyeing existing garments, rather than buying new ones. Photographs of crowds at the Festival of Britain in 1951 and in nationwide Coronation celebrations in 1953 tend to bear out this point. People are trying hard to look their best, with the men still far from free from the short-back-and-sides-and-shiny-boots regime of their Services years, yet their clothes are evidently long-term possessions, veterans of any number of post-war weddings, christenings and job interviews.

All this was excellent news for Bollom, and ambitious companies like them. In 1950 the 200th shop was opened, and in spite of rising wages and increased competition the company was able to pay shareholders a regular 50 per cent dividend from the end of the war until the mid-1950s. There was further responsibility for Philip Bollom in 1953, when his brief was extended to oversight of the Cardiff works – but his elevation to the board in 1954 was by no means the happy event he and his family might have imagined it would be.

Later that year his father Ivor suffered a severe heart attack. For three decades he had been the company's driving force, generating the kind of wealth that had given his family a happy and comfortable lifestyle and provided secure employment to hundreds of others. Yet his assets, by and large, were tied up in the company, and it was with some trepidation that his family realised that had he died in 1954, they would have had to sell his interests in the business to pay estate duties. Family firms were a time-honoured tradition, and Bollom was a prime example of one that had achieved almost spectacular success; yet the message of 1954 was that commercial life was growing ever more complex, and assumptions that could have been made by previous generations no longer necessarily applied in post-war Britain. Ivor Bollom's illness, which he happily survived, had been a salutary experience.

While he was convalescing, and by coincidence, an agent approached the company with the news that a large national concern was interested in a takeover. It was not a new story, but while all previous offers had been consigned to the waste paper basket, the directors decided to take this one further. The interested company was Johnson Brothers Ltd., which had become the world's largest dry cleaning company through self-generated growth and a record of amicable takeovers that was well known throughout the industry. Led by their chairman, Douglas Crockatt, they soon entered into serious negotiations with the Bollom family in London, a process speeded considerably by the mutual admiration shared by Mr. Crockatt and Ivor Bollom.

Talks went on through the autumn of 1954, at a time when Bollom shilling shares were quoted at around three shillings each on the Bristol stock exchange. In 1977 Mr. Sam Bollom's recollection of events was as follows: "They offered us 3s. 3d. for a shilling share, then 4s., then 5s., and when it reached 6s. a share we thought we should inform the shareholders. Finally we sold out to Johnson at 6s. 3d. a share." There were a million of these shilling shares, plus 36,000 preference shares for which Johnson offered 21s. each. The Bollom family felt that terms like these would be unlikely to be matched in the foreseeable future and accepted them, at the same time recommending them to other shareholders.

It was the end of an era, bringing the retirement of Ivor Bollom, his brothers Fred and Sam and two other senior directors. Ivor had acquired the tailoring firm Cole and Pottow as a Bollom sideline in 1943, and now, eager for the stimulus of commercial life to the last, he bought it back from the firm as a retirement interest. His company went into the Johnson Group with his elder son as managing director and Philip as general manager with a seat on the Bollom board, but it was not long before David was making his mark at national level, and Philip Bollom's day would come, too. From now on his destiny lay not with the family firm at home in Bristol, but with a nationwide company with its roots in the North. Not just any company, either; if you are going to be given the chance to aim for the top in a business, there is no harm in its being the biggest of its type in the world . . .

5 — *The Pioneering Years*

The company joined by Bollom of Bristol in 1955 could trace its roots back to 1817 – a wonderful record of service, but one that was by no means unique in the wider Johnson Group. Eastman and Son, a member of the Associated Dyers and Cleaners combine taken over in 1938, stemmed from a shop in London's Tottenham Court Road which opened in 1802; Pullars of Perth, the dominant Associated Dyers company, was only seven years Johnson's junior, with a history stretching back to 1824; and two years after the Bollom purchase the group took in Joseph Harris Ltd. of Birmingham, the most senior of them all with records stretching back to 1780. This firm grew out of a workshop opened in an orchard by one John Varney just four years after the American colonies were lost by George III's troops in the War of Independence, and almost a decade before the French Revolution; not that either event is known to have had any noticeable effect on Varney's business.

All these companies were established before the invention of dry or chemical cleaning, which is generally credited to a Frenchman, Jean-Baptiste Jolly, who was born in the Seine-et-Oise department and moved to Paris to work in around 1800. Like so many who have made their mark in the industry since, he was a young man of no great academic background who progressed by prolific hard work, bright ideas and a sound marketing sense. He found work in the Bellin dyehouse on the Rue de Tracy, and when the owner retired in 1807 he had accumulated sufficient funds to take it over. This was quite a breakthrough for him – but it did not come close to his turn of good fortune some 18 years later, in 1825, when an accident in his home led him to his momentous discovery. A maid in his house upset a paraffin lamp over a coloured tablecloth. When it dried, Jolly was intrigued to find that it looked cleaner than it had done since new, with several apparently permanent stains purged away. One of the problems facing dyers at that time, all of whom used natural pigments based on vegetable products, was that before a fabric could be treated it had to be cleaned thoroughly. Dyes were unable to penetrate grease or dirt, so would not take to dirty cloth; this was all very well if the fabric could be washed efficiently in the normal manner, but if it could not, then satisfactory dyeing was out of the question.

Jolly realised that the accident with the lamp had opened up new possibilities, an alternative method of cleaning which might allow him to dye a wider range of fabrics. After much experimenting he devised a manual dry cleaning method using the powerful benzine, a hydrocarbon mixture allied to paraffin; this process, while revolutionary and effective for its day, seems prohibitively laborious and expensive to modern eyes. The main problem lay in the fact that as the garment was dipped in the benzine the dirt would simply be redeposited elsewhere, making for unacceptably patchy and uneven cleaning. Jolly's solution was to unpick the seams to divide the garment carefully into sections, dip each piece into bowls of benzine separately, brush and dry them in a hot room and then sew them together again. This was the "French cleaning" that kept its mystique for so long in the eyes of the public, perhaps not least because it was promoted heavily in this country by companies with French names for many years after the process had been abandoned. Only since the last war has "French cleaning" ceased to have an impact on the national consciousness.

All this Gallic ingenuity failed to make any mark on the British scene until 1866, when Jolly's grandson and a team of skilled workers from Paris moved in to Perth to teach Pullars the art of dry cleaning. John Pullar and his sons Robert and James were greatly impressed, and straightaway began to adapt machinery to put dry cleaning on the same mechanised basis as their dyeing process. Not that it was an altogether inviting prospect. The early machines were clumsy and inconvenient, the solvent was famously inflammable, and it was not long before the factory inspectors caught on to the possible hazards. Stringent regulations ordering that all dry cleaning should be done in buildings separated from other processes slowed its development before the First World War, leaving it as little more than a sideline of the dyeing trade. Not until the introduction of the Burtol cleaning unit to Britain in the early 1930s – the breakthrough that coincided so happily with the early years of the Bollom company in Bristol – did the industry take off.

We shall look more fully at the history of Pullars later in the book, but before we leave them here we must note their part in another revolution in the dyeing industry. In 1856 William Perkin, an 18-year-old student at the Royal College of Chemistry, mixed the coal tar product aniline with bichromate of potash while researching a means of producing quinine artificially. The result of his efforts was no drug for the treatment of fevers but a rich and brilliant hue – the first artificial dye in the world – that would soon take Paris by storm as mauve, named after the French for the mallow flower. From 1859 it took on an even more Gallic flavour when Empress Eugénie named it magenta after the battle in Lombardy in which her nation's forces combined with Sardinia to defeat Austria in the struggle for Italian independence; but for the teenage Perkin in 1856 such triumphs still lay ahead. What he needed was an interested dyer to help test his product on a commercial scale, and in the young Sir Robert Pullar he found an enthusiastic and practically helpful ally. There is a well known story of the two – Robert was some ten years older, at 28 – dyeing the Pullar family bath purple while experimenting with lengths of silk; but for all his expertise as a dyer, Robert Pullar was not a dye-maker, and he met nothing but stubborn resistance when he tried to interest British manufacturers in his friend's discovery. Eventually Perkin went to Europe with his formula, selling it to a German company, and it was the chintzes, cottons and silks of the Paris fashions that made it a household name. "Mauve on, please," comic policemen would growl in music hall sketches of the late 1850s, and it was the French name that stuck. The fact nevertheless remains that the first use of aniline dye, the initial important step in organic chemistry, was by Pullars of Perth. The company lost no time in sending a length of silk to Queen Victoria, and one of the earliest samples can be seen at Perth Museum to this day.

By this stage of the century the Johnson dyeing business in Liverpool was already into its second generation. The first shop, in Ranelagh Street, was established by one William Arnold in 1817 and bought twelve years later by William Johnson, who added woollen and other cloths to Arnold's speciality of silk. William had been a dyer in Leeds with his elder brother, members of a family who had carried on the trade in York since at least 1500. It was their father Edward, a hard-drinking press-setter turned Methodist convert, who had left York for a better life in Leeds; William, in turn, was persuaded that more opportunities lay for him west of the Pennines in Liverpool, where his brother-in-law Thomas Sands, a future mayor of the city, was a young and successful cotton merchant. In 1811 William and his wife Jane named their first son after her brother, and Sands remains a family Christian name to this day. Another fascinating link with those earliest days of the company is the fact that the Ranelagh Street shop remains a Johnson Brothers unit, its basement still showing evidence of the original dyehouse.

Thomas Sands Johnson joined his father's business in Liverpool after working for McGill of London – later to amalgamate with Eastman – and with his uncle in Leeds. He was unhappily to die in 1843 at the age of 32, but he left the business a remarkable asset in the shape of his wife Eliza, two years his senior. A Warrington girl, she did not let the fact that she had five sons aged under ten stand in the way of her throwing herself energetically into the commercial world along with her father-in-law, who came out of retirement after Thomas's death, and her late husband's younger half-brother, another William. At this stage she and her boys were living above the Johnsons' second shop, in Bold Street.

She was very much the dominant force and in 1849, two years before the first William's death, she dissolved the partnership with her brother-in-law, who riposted by setting up in opposition lower down Bold Street. It was not a happy move on his part, for when he died intestate in 1866 he left debts of £111 1s. 1d. against assets of £63 13s. Eliza, however, flourished. Ranelagh Street steamed with tubs and coppers full of wood dyes, yellow from tropical American fustic and black from logwood, while great glass carboys held spirit for dyeing and fixing everything from French merino dresses to costly Canton crepe shawls and ribbons by the thousand. By 1853 Mrs. Johnson was directing building work for an extension at the back of the premises.

Her eldest son, Thomas Sands Johnson like his father, was born in 1834, and like him, too, when he was 15 he was apprenticed for five years to McGill and Eastman. He scarcely found the streets of London paved with gold; indeed, Eliza had to pay a premium of £150 to McGill, as well as finding the boy's keep in the capital, and he carried lasting memories of 14-hour days Monday to Saturday, and the particular torture of plunging his arms in vats of cold dye on winter mornings to process cotton linings. No doubt he was delighted when she called him home to Liverpool a year early in 1853 to help in an expansion of the business that brought new shops in Chester, Preston and Warrington and necessitated a move to a larger factory in Celia Street, Kirkdale in 1861; Ranelagh Street stayed on as a receiving shop.

In spite of its urban sounding name, Celia Street was out in the countryside, with wild roses growing in the hedgerows. A less salubrious attraction was a clear view across to the local gaol, and when there was a hanging the dyehouse's dozen workmen would knock off early to see the show. Bathing in the two clear ponds close to the works provided less controversial pleasure, but it seems that there was an element of the Wild West in this remote spot, and when young Thomas carried the wages from his home in Bottle Lane to the works on Friday nights he took the precaution of carrying what was euphemistically termed a life-preserver. In spite of this, the Kirkdale development was his pride and joy. He drew loving plans of his family's "steam dyeing and bleaching works" in a little leather-bound notebook – and more important for the future of the business, he and his mother soon saw the advantages of having large and expansible factory premises serving growing numbers of receiving shops. It was the Johnsons' first lesson in a principle which would eventually establish them as world leaders in their field.

In 1858 Thomas married Margaret Jane Corlett, the daughter of a missionary in Antigua. She became a noted Nonconformist speaker and charity worker and the family still gives her credit for the public speaking skills of her son Benjamin Sands and her grandson Thomas Benjamin Sands – Sir Ben and Mr. Tom to future generations of Johnson employees. Benjamin Sands (b. 1865), Frederick Corlett (b. 1870) and Thomas Sands III (b. 1874) were the three Johnson brothers from whom the limited liability company took its name when it was founded in 1898. They made a formidable team, and their efforts helped lay the foundations of the international group we know today.

6 — *Sir Ben and His Brothers*

Young Ben Johnson was not subjected to the formal apprenticeship in dyeing undergone by his father and grandfather; it was becoming increasingly clear that a grasp of retail trade was a greater asset to the head of a service industry such as this than an intimate knowledge of cold-dyeing cotton linings and in 1881, when he was 16, Ben was plunged into the commercial deep end by being put in charge of the family's Preston branch. He travelled there daily, and for the rest of his life he refused to be immersed in a head office view of the world, always remembering those "in the field". He became a partner with his father in 1889, and chairman and managing director of the limited company founded in the three brothers' name nine years later.

His fifty-plus years of service to the company were matched by a distinguished public career lasting almost as long; in the years since his time a succession of senior Johnson executives has found a place on the judicial bench and Sir Ben set this trend, serving as both a justice of the peace for Bootle and a county magistrate. He was twice mayor of Bootle before he was 30, and his knighthood in 1910 came when he was just 45. The First World War saw his appointment as director-general of the Royal Army clothing department, and later his promotion to the even more important role of director-general of National Factories. A Deputy Lieutenant and High Sheriff of Lancashire and a hard worker for the Liberal Party in the North-west, he was prominent on church and hospital committees in the Liverpool area, as well as serving on the city's university council for three years. Liverpool University honoured him with the degree of doctor of law in 1931, six years before his death.

Not that all his good works were held up for the world to see. His private philanthropy was something he kept very private indeed, but one way in which his abiding interest in people in general and his workforce in particular was allowed to show was his habit of hanging many of his valuable paintings in the offices and workrooms of the factory in Mildmay Road, Bootle, that was opened with the launch of the limited company. There were more than a hundred there at the time of his death, and it was only a small way in which he helped raise the sights and the standard of living of the people around him. Such gestures sometimes took on a slightly eccentric air. His nephew Tom Johnson swears that when he was out touring the branches he was known to reward a hard-working assistant or manageress with a string of pearls. Another time, when he was looking for possible new shops in the Plymouth area, he had been standing round a jeweller's weighing it up for so long that a policeman came up and asked him what he was doing. "You see that clock?" said Sir Ben. "Do you like it?" The P.C. admitted that he did, and before he knew it he was taking it home as a gift. This was perhaps a rather expensive way to prove to a policeman that one had far too much money to be contemplating robbing a jeweller's shop, but on another occasion Sir Ben was obliged to keep his wallet in his pocket. Taking coffee in a café one afternoon he was touched by the sight of a down-at-heel old crone a few tables away. "Waitress," he said, "I'd like to pay for that lady over there." "I wouldn't if I were you," came the dusty reply. "She's a millionairess."

Not that a portrait of an energetic, dutiful and talented businessman and pillar of society pays sufficient tribute to Sir Ben. "He was so dynamic," says his nephew Tom Johnson, chairman from 1966 to 1975. "People just flocked around him. He had seven shops when he started, and 700 when he died – and that was only part of the story. A few years ago John Crockatt, who followed me as chairman, unearthed one of his policy documents, and apart from the archaic language it was couched in it might have been drawn up by any enlightened employer today. He revelled in exchanging ideas with many of the great pioneers of industrial welfare, companies like Lever Brothers of Port Sunlight, Cadbury, Rowntree and Theodore Taylor of Batley, in which the Quaker influence was often strong. Combined with this was his tremendous capacity for getting things done. I remember once being down in Hereford with him and his chairman designate, Oswald Gunnell, looking at a shop. We had arranged to see it at 2p.m., and as we were finishing lunch Gunnell, who was no slouch himself, said: 'Come on, then, let's go.' 'No need,' said Uncle. 'I bought it this morning.' We'd scarcely split up for more than five minutes, and he'd done it all.

"There's a famous story about Bill Shankly, the single-minded football manager who laid the foundations for Liverpool's success, celebrating his wedding anniversary by taking his wife to see Accrington Stanley Reserves. I think the tale of Ben Johnson's honeymoon in Bournemouth tops that. He opened five shops while he was down South. Well, all right, he didn't actually open them, but he laid down how they should be altered and staffed, and got the railway timetable to Bootle sorted out." No doubt his bride Netta took it with a smile. She must have known by then the kind of man she had married; above all, he had a mountainous capacity to inspire affection, devotion and respect, and that was the way in which he was viewed not just through the eyes of his immediate family but by thousands in Bootle and far beyond.

The second brother, Mr. Fred, entered the business in 1889 and became a director and its first secretary on its formation as a limited company. Quiet and exact, he remained a devoted servant of the company, never missing a meeting until his last illness, and his honesty and caution proved valued assets as Johnson Brothers spread their net ever-wider. He certainly watched the firm's pennies. "Every quarter when the branches sent in their electricity bills he would go through them assiduously and compare them with previous ones," Tom Johnson recalls. "Once he wrote back to a manageress saying: 'You've changed the lamp in the back room to a higher wattage; change it back'." Tom's son Sands has a story on the same theme: "Not long ago I was looking at some plans for the alteration of a shop in the 1920s. They showed two lights, one above the counter and one in the back, together with the wattage. In each case these figures had been crossed out and lower ones substituted in a firm, neat hand. I couldn't swear that it was Fred's writing, but there was no doubt who was behind it." Tom Johnson believes that this rigorous policy continued until after the last war, to no good effect: "One day a chap came up to me and said: 'I can always find your shops, they're so badly lit. I just look down the street, spot the dingiest looking one and there you are, Johnsons.' Well, you can imagine, that was it. We had strip lighting in before you knew it." Like his elder brother, Fred was a great lover of paintings and a patron of the arts, though cricket was probably his greatest passion. He died in 1944, and not many people around Bootle Cricket Club remember him now, but for many a decade he was a much loved figure in the pavilion or out on the square.

The third brother, Thomas Sands III or more usually Mr. Sands, came to the company in remarkable fashion. He was nine years Ben's junior, and when the time came for him to leave school his two elder brothers felt there was no room for him in the business – a reminder

Top: Bristol area manageresses' dinner in 1944, a reminder that both in peace and war, the dry cleaning industry is overwhelmingly dependent on women workers.

Bottom: the Bollom Victory Tour to Cheddar and Weston-super-Mare in August 1945. Sam Bollom is in the foreground behind the little girl, David is behind him in spectacles, and Ivor is slightly to the right in a coloured open-necked shirt that drew veiled comment in *The Bollom Letter's* report of the great day.

An early link with the United States, a Bollom fact-finding visit to the Prosperity Company of Syracuse, New York, in 1947. Ivor and director Percy Radford are seated centre and right, while standing second from the left is Fred Bollom.

"Is This London's Finest Dry Cleaning Depot?" The rhetorical question was asked by a leading trade journal shortly after this unit branch opened in Kensington High Street in 1947.

Life at Bollom's Horfield Road factory in 1954, the year before the company joined the Johnson Group. Top left, darning stockings; top right, fuelling the boiler; bottom left, reshaping hats; and bottom right, loading a cleaning machine.

More scenes from Horfield Road, 1954. Top left, repairs in the capable hands of Bobby Williams; top right, cleaning carpets; and below, adding that final hand-pressed touch to fashionable full skirts.

that Victorian family firms were not always the automatic meal ticket for life that disgruntled workers might sometimes have imagined them to be. Sands' response to this challenge was to sign on as a worker in the dyehouse, at which Ben and Fred relented and sent him to Yorkshire College, later to become Leeds University, to study chemistry and dyeing. Back at Kirkdale he set up a small laboratory, but his brief was soon extended and in due course he became works manager. The 1898 relaunch saw him appointed a director and general manager, though when he died at the tragically early age of 47 in 1921 he was joint managing director. Sands Johnson was an all-rounder whose technical knowledge was backed by sound judgment, breadth of outlook and a sense of justice and integrity that made him a wise and sympathetic employer. His death left a great void in the company, yet in two ways at least his contribution to its continued wellbeing emulated that of his more renowned eldest brother. His first great triumph was in bringing a fellow Leeds student, Oswald Gunnell, to the company; he was drafted in to take charge of the laboratory at Bootle, but by 1933 he had risen to the heights of managing director, and he eventually made it all the way and became chairman. Mr. Sands' other masterstroke was to stand the company in good stead into the next generation and beyond. Sir Ben did not leave a son to carry on the family name; his youngest brother and his wife had just the one boy, born in 1910, but as we shall record later, Thomas Benjamin Sands Johnson was to go on to make his own indelible mark on the company.

Before the limited company was formed the firm had not always found it easy to keep abreast of a fast-changing business. By the late 1870s and 1880s it was no longer a matter of simple processing, using natural dyes for a limited range of articles and "four gallons of benzine bought from a chemist" for what little dry cleaning was done. Perkin's aniline breakthrough had led to new and lively competition in the market, and the dictates of fashion meant that far from a staple diet of silk, cotton and wool, dyers found themselves meeting the challenge of everything from feathers to cretonne and muslin. It must be confessed that there was another reason why the company at that time ran into what would today be termed cash-flow difficulties. The brothers' father, Thomas, was a heavy drinker who ran up debts to an alarming extent, no doubt believing that the success Ben was making of the business gave him scope to splash out a little. The final straw came one afternoon when a customer came in to settle a bill for £20, a vast sum in the 1880s. He made the mistake of paying the money to Thomas, and the next morning there was scarcely any of it left. That was enough for Ben, who took out an advertisement in the press to the effect that no future bills should be settled with his father. This was the background to the decision made in 1889, nine years before the limited company option bore fruit, to borrow £430 from the brothers' uncle John Labron Johnson, a prominent Liverpool solicitor. It took 14 years to discharge the debt, and when the last instalment was paid Sir Ben was so proud that he had the cancelled I.O.U. framed and hung in his office for the rest of his days.

1889 was the year in which Sir Ben went into partnership with his father; the staff at Kirkdale at that time numbered just 21, while seven receiving shops took the total workforce up to 56. In the next seven years, however, some 56 new receiving depots followed, and it was this sudden and quite unprecedented expansion of business that led to the foundations of the new Mildmay Road plant to be laid in 1896. By the turn of the century the new limited company was set fair to capitalise on improved dyeing methods pioneered by Jolly, while Mr. Sands' small laboratory at Kirkdale had led to the development of a patented frame dyeing technique that was to serve the company well for nearly half a century. Later, Oswald Gunnell's larger lab at Bootle set the pace for a programme of chemical analysis, experimental dyeing, safety tests and checks on the effects of solvents on fabrics and colours that continues unabated to this day. Such work was to become a keynote of the industry in the twentieth century, and thanks to Gunnell and his team Johnson Brothers found themselves at the forefront of the field.

By 1908 there were 250 branches, compared with 46 in 1895. When Ben was knighted he addressed nearly a thousand workers at Bootle, reminded them of a further thousand out in the field, and reminisced on the 56 who formed the total workforce when he became a partner 21 years previously. "Everyone knows that nearly 2,000 knights and ladies have been created by the honour bestowed upon me," he told them. "And if the King himself only knew, he would be very pleased." Those 2,000 were soon swelled by further new branches and by the enlargement of the Mildmay Road factory, while drivers were added to the payroll with the much-heralded arrival of the firm's first motor delivery van, a Ford with solid tyres and a horn shaped like a bugle. New boilers added a 400,000-brick chimney to the neighbourhood, Lord Derby opened a large new building in the year of Ben's knighthood, and by 1914 a modern receiving and packing shed was soon followed by an improved boiler house. An enlarged dyehouse had to wait until 1920, and that was not the only repercussion of the First World War. Until then Germany had been the main source of aniline dyes and now, at last, British manufacturers were forced to sit up and take notice of Perkin's discovery of some 60 years earlier. But there was still room for new ideas, and just as Pullars had called in Jolly's expertise in the 1860s, during the wartime years Johnson recruited experts in invisible mending or "French darning" from the Continent to teach five of their girls this intricate craft. The company had adopted the slogan New Lamps For Old as its trademark in 1911, and by the end of the wartime years it was putting the concept in practice in a variety of ways that would have bewildered the industrious Eliza back in Ranelagh Street in the 1840s.

There was one other way in which the company could grow, however – and grow quickly. That was by acquisition of and amalgamation with other firms, a process that would bring not only a network of branches in parts of the country hitherto unconquered, but a whole new dimension of factory plant and potential management expertise. The 250 branches of 1908 had become 350 by 1914, but the war reduced this expansion to a trickle, no more than five new openings in as many years. With the return of peace and the high hopes of lasting prosperity that came with it, the directors looked upon the amalgamation option with renewed urgency. They rather liked the look of two other progressive family concerns, Jas. Smith and Sons of Dewsbury, West Yorkshire and Flinn and Son of Brighton, both of which had progressed considerably since their foundation in the 1850s. By lucky chance, Smith and Flinn equally liked the look of the Bootle set-up, a deal was struck, and the Johnson Group was born. It was a happy and confident Sir Ben who conducted the young Prince of Wales around the Bootle works in 1921, the factory girls in their bright clean aprons cheering him to the echo.

7 — *Pulling Together*

The early years of amalgamation were not easy for the Johnson, Smith and Flinn companies, or indeed for the London-based Lush and Cook Ltd., who joined them in 1928. It soon became clear that hopes of a boom in the wake of the Armistice had been sadly misguided, and a combination of the depression and competition more fierce than ever before was enough to set the alarm bells ringing. When a new duty was imposed on petrol and cleaning spirits in the 1930s there was nothing for it but to dismiss staff and close plants, but as so often happens in such grim circumstances, some gold was raked out of the ashes. In the North-west Johnson Brothers met the challenge of the public simply not being able to pay for cleaning by reducing their prices by one third. This led to a reorganisation and rationalisation of the Mildmay Road factory from top to bottom, with conveyors to carry goods from department to department. Heavy basketwork hampers were replaced by cardboard and fibre cartons, and a keen deal was hammered out with the railway companies to carry these containers from branches as far apart as Penzance and Stirling. It was another triumph for Sir Ben and the increasingly influential Oswald Gunnell, and before the grand old man died further improvements had been made to a staff welfare scheme of which the company had been proud since the early years of the century. Staff welfare and relations remain high on the Johnson Group agenda, as will be noted later in this book.

There were more acquisitions, John Crockatt of Leeds in 1935 – a move that was to have a profound effect on the future Johnson Group management structure – and the big Eastman/Pullars/Stevenson Associated Dyers and Cleaners combine in 1938. Sir Ben Johnson died on Christmas Day, 1937, aged 72 and with nearly 57 years in the business behind him, but with the purchase of the Crockatt company he had mapped out the group's senior management structure for decades to come. "I remember my uncle calling me in and explaining his desire to buy Crockatt's to me," Tom Johnson recalls. "He reasoned that with Oswald Gunnell then in his fifties and me in my twenties, the company would need a chairman to take the reins between his retirement and my maturity. In Douglas Crockatt, who was just under 40 at the time, he had recognised 'a big man in a small company', and as usual, he was right." As it turned out, a combination of the Second World War and an acute reluctance to step down meant that Oswald Gunnell did not depart until well after his official retirement age, in 1952, by which time Douglas Crockatt was 56 and Tom Johnson a far from callow 42. Mr. Crockatt, in turn, stayed on until he was 70 and it was not until 1966, more than 30 years after being confirmed as the next chairman but one by his uncle, that Mr. Tom finally made it to the top. Nonetheless, the fact remains that in that conversation of 1935 Ben Johnson mapped out the group's leadership for the next 40 years.

Oswald Gunnell replaced Sir Ben as chairman; the assiduous Mr. Fred continued for another seven years as company secretary, and it seems that his careful ways with money rubbed off on the new man at the top. Reminiscing in 1970, Denis Smith, another group stalwart, said of Oswald Gunnell: "He would always scrutinise any expense from every angle to see if it could be reduced, and would haggle over £5 in the rent for a seven-year lease renewal. A £5 reduction was £35 in our pockets, not the landlords'. He welcomed every leap year almost with glee, because 'we had one more day's trade at every shop for the same rent, and one more day's service from every salary-earner for the same salary'."

By this time, too, of course, the next generation of the family was making its presence felt in the form of Mr. Tom, and the company felt that this sense of familiarity and continuity was particularly important in seeing it and its workers through the Second World War, in which Liverpool suffered at least as much as any Northern city. The signs at the beginning of the war had not been as dire as they had been in 1914. Lessons learned then meant that the industry in Britain no longer depended upon Germany for its dyestuffs – but that earlier conflict had brought nothing like the pounding that the Germans were now handing out to Liverpool docks and their surroundings night after night, and twice in the early May of 1941, on Saturday the 3rd and the following Wednesday, the Mildmay Road works received direct hits. On the first night the Luftwaffe's prize scalp in the area was the Bryant and May match factory – and the phosphorus stores were still glowing like a beacon for their aircraft when they came over again mid-week. This second raid, which destroyed two complete buildings, was particularly demoralising.

The departments for recovering eiderdowns, dressmaking, packing, printing and window displays, as well as the canteen, had sunk without trace in a sea of splintered glass and rubble. For those who were first on the scene it seemed like the end of the world, yet within a fortnight the wheels of production were turning again, and the show was back on the road.

Out in the branches it was a similar tale of direct hits and narrow escapes, tragedy, heroism and sheer hard slog. In the last year of the war, which brought the great doodlebug offensive in the South, no fewer than 51 of the group's shops were damaged by bombs or rockets in the London area alone. In other ways, too, the pattern of work was disrupted. As more and more skilled and experienced men and women left for the Forces or the munitions factories their places were taken by raw part-timers or school-leavers too young to serve, and it took time for them to pick up the threads. Nevertheless, the importance of dyeing and cleaning was stressed when it was declared an essential industry, and as with Bollom down in Bristol, Johnson Brothers and their partner companies found that life had never been busier as they served the needs of both the Forces and a civilian population increasingly determined to make do and mend. Workers reflected the spirit of the times by joining Air Raid Precautions or the Home Guard, fire-watching or serving in the special police, collecting salvage, supporting National Savings, Digging for Victory or knitting for the troops. The dyeing and cleaning industry generally has always prided itself on its camaraderie and team spirit, but never has it been so apparent as between the years 1939 and 1945.

Normal life did not resume quickly in the post-war years. Men poured back to the factories from overseas, but in many cases all was not as they had left it, and they were forced to draw on all the reserves of patience and good humour they had built up in the Forces. At Bootle the basement of the office block had been strengthened as a shelter; 200 people huddled in it, and were glad to do so, in that nightmarish May of 1941, but now it was 1946, and it was time it was restored for everyday use. It was the same in the carpet department, which had spent the war as a decontamination centre; and as for the buildings destroyed, not until 1957 did the company finally make good all that had been lost in those surreal two nights of bombing.

Change was coming thick and fast in other directions. On June 30, 1952 Oswald Gunnell retired after 56 years' service, almost exactly equalling his predecessor Sir Ben Johnson's record – and within two weeks he had died. His place as chairman was at last taken by Douglas Crockatt, who had been head-hunted by Sir Ben 17 years previously, and he held the post for 14 eventful years until 1966. As has been noted, Mr. Crockatt, a First World War machine-gunner who was mentioned in despatches, was in his mid-50s when he took the reins, with more than 30 years' top-level experience behind him as joint managing director and later chairman of the company founded by his father John in Yorkshire in 1875. The Crockatts were linked by marriage to the Pullar family, and dye was in their blood, but to this instinctive feel for and love of the business Douglas Crockatt added a shrewd, energetic, imaginative but always scrupulously honourable business sense that was to stand the wider Johnson Group in good stead in its crucial years of post-war change, and his sons John and Allan, brother Arthur and nephew Norman would also go on to serve the company well. Like several in the chair before and since him, his roots were in Nonconformism and Liberal politics – Westminster's loss was the cleaning industry's gain when he failed to be elected M.P. for York in 1929 – and his interests again echoed Sir Ben's in his long and distinguished service as a J.P. in Leeds and a member of the city's university council; in 1968 Leeds awarded him the honorary degree of doctor of law, which once more drew a parallel with Sir Ben's award from Liverpool in 1931. He had immense and demanding interests in the greater world of finance, as a long-serving director of the Leeds Permanent Building Society – president from 1956 to '59 – and as a member of the Yorkshire Insurance Company board, where he was deputy chairman from 1962 to '71.

After leaving the Johnson Group in 1966 he spent four busy years as head office director of the General Accident Corporation, till he finally accepted the idea of retirement at the age of 75 in 1971. Within the trade he spent the height of the depression years, from 1931 to '34, as president of the National Federation of Dyers and Cleaners, and from 1937 he was a liveryman of the Dyers' Company, serving in the key role of prime warden in 1965. Amid all this he found time to play tough, competitive Yorkshire club cricket until well into his fifties – and more important, to make a point of keeping in close personal touch with his workforce, often spending an hour before breakfast to write to those he knew had problems in his small, neat hand. "A business is much more than a pile of assets – bricks and mortar, machinery and dry figures," he once declared. "A business consists essentially of people working together for a common end, and we forget it at our peril." It is the Johnson Group's great good fortune to have had a succession of senior executives before and since who have shared this view and made it central to the company's philosophy. Douglas Crockatt enjoyed a long and happy retirement, and he was 84 when he died at his country home near Wetherby in April 1980.

There were other significant changes at around this time. In 1953 a separate firm, Johnson Brothers (Dyers) Properties Ltd. was formed to take the responsibility of seeking new premises in key shopping areas and managing existing branches, for dry cleaning, rather than dyeing, was now very much the group's prime concern. Under Douglas Crockatt also in the mid to late 1950s came a period of revolution in the industry, of intense competition and unprecedented change within the Johnson Group. At last it was time to take off and lay to rest the hardships of the war years, though it was evident that the process would not always be pleasant and easy; such was the mood of the company when Philip Bollom's family elected to come into the fold in 1955.

8 — *We Have Lift-Off*

Hard on the heels of the Bollom merger came the acquisition of Joseph Harris of Birmingham with its 85 branches in 1957, and the Bird Group of Newcastle-upon-Tyne, including Harton Cleaners and Dyers, in 1959. There was particular piquancy in the Harris purchase, for Douglas Crockatt had first met the company's chairman, Herbert Harris, as a machine-gunner in France during the First World War. By now a combination of this rapid expansion and razor-sharp competition from outside had convinced the directors that a programme of hard rationalisation was necessary, and in 1960 the holding company Johnson Group Cleaners Ltd. was formed. As before, each associated company retained its own identity and board of directors, but with member firms finding themselves increasingly in competition with each other in valuable high street premises up and down the country, the need to divide the territory more logically and advantageously had grown painfully obvious.

In Bollom's trading area, for instance, there were also shops belonging to Johnson Brothers, Pullars of Perth, who were still transporting orders up to Scotland from the length and breadth of Britain, Lush and Cook, Eastman and Flinn. Though the Johnson group had been a historical fact since 1920, no great thought had been put to this question in the past, and when the nettle had to be grasped in the late 1950s not all directors up and down the country welcomed the idea. Many remembered their own and their forbears' struggles to build up business and extend their territory, and hated the thought of all that effort simply being signed away on a piece of paper; others found it hard to see beyond the simple equation of fewer branches for our company means smaller takings for our company, ignoring the impact of such a move on wider group profits; and all of them, such is the nature of the business and the people in it, dreaded the thought of telling loyal staff that their services were no longer required.

The reason why such a move had not been made earlier lay largely in the fact that profits for all had been healthy enough not to warrant any drastic surgery, but the trading conditions of the late 1950s and early 1960s put an end to that. The development of non-inflammable cleaning solvents opened the door for scores of small operators to cash in on an industry showing an average growth rate of 10 per cent a year and start their own small cleaning units, a world away from the old Burtols of the early 1930s in safety and efficiency; not surprisingly, the makers of new cleaning machinery were only too happy to help them on their way with a variety of attractive package deals. Suddenly the conveyor equipment so ingeniously installed at Bootle by Oswald Gunnell just a decade earlier began to look like something out of the Ark, carrying the clothes from the white spirit cleaning machines through examining, finishing, packing and despatch. Those huge machines, extractors, stoves, travelling conveyors; they stood in factories like Mildmay Road like monuments to industry, built to last perhaps for ever, with regular and devoted maintenance; now small businessmen on street corners could buy a single sleek machine on the H.P., plug it in and reduce a process that had previously taken two and a half hours to 25 minutes.

It was a new challenge to the Johnson companies, and it was clear that they, too, would have to experiment with unit shops in their drive for rationalisation. Until now any modernisation of shops had tended to be restricted to making the reception area more bright and pleasant, hitting upon attractive advertising and promotional formulae and catering for the comparatively recent system of returning clothes from the factory to the customer on wire hangers, but it was now plain that something more was required. Tom Johnson recalls a visit to Chicago in 1958: "I was in a unit shop when a lady came in and said 'I don't like the way you've pressed this dress'. The manager said 'come on through and show the girl how you want it done'. Not long afterwards I was in our branch in Marylebone High Street when a man came in and said he did not like the way we had pressed his lapels. The girl at the counter was just as polite as the American manager had been – but all she could offer was to send the jacket back to Bootle and return it in a week's time. I thought 'we're not in the same business as the Americans'." This led to a rationalisation of transport that ended a decades-old reliance on the railway and put every branch within a van's drive of its nearest factory, often through transfer from one group company to another. Johnson Brothers, for instance, lost some 250 shops bearing their name in this way, almost all in the South, while in the North-west the company broke the receiving shops and factory mould that had stood them in good stead for 121 years when they opened their first unit shop advertising One Hour Garment Cleaning in Princess Street, Bury in 1960. Several other companies in the group had had unit shops to supplement their factories since the Burtol revolution of 1932, but up until this time Johnson Brothers had held to the feeling that the works system, with its tried and trusted methods and existing plant, would continue to play a central part in large cleaners' operations. With the break-through in safe solvents it was obvious that this view would have to be revised, but with unit machines selling at around £10,000 each in 1960 there was no way that hundreds of branches would be converted overnight, even had their premises been suitable, and there was still heavy investment in old-established and new factories. Many of these have since been closed now that unit cleaning is a fact of life, but the growing field of textile rental has breathed new life into those that remain.

The rationalisation gave market areas based broadly on television advertising zones, though there was an element of overlap. For Bollom, where Tom Johnson was chairman, David Bollom managing director and Philip Bollom general manager, this meant control of central Southern England and the South-west, with some 200 shops and factories at Bristol and Bournemouth. A separate company, Johnson Cleaners (South West) Ltd., was formed to run two more factories and 132 branches in Devon, Cornwall and South Wales with the same management structure. Although experimental unit shops sprang up through this region in the early 1960s the Bournemouth and Cardiff factories were both modernised extensively, and a new plant was opened in Plymouth at a cost of £60,000. By 1964 Bollom and Johnson South West had reduced their branches to 304, with an annual turnover of around £700,000.

The 1955 merger had worked well for the Bollom brothers. They liked Tom Johnson, the warm, cheerful and dedicated Lancastrian now at the helm of their company, who called down to see them a couple of days every month. Tom Johnson's recollections of those early days are also happy, though he gives himself credit for giving the two young West Countrymen a few lessons in hard-headed Northern ways: "It was obvious that when they were looking for new premises to rent for branches they were used to meeting the agents' asking price. They'd be asked, say, £200 a year, and if they thought that seemed reasonable they'd take it. 'Argue,' I'd say. 'Knock them down £10, £20, £100.' At one time we had about 80 shops with their rent coming up for review, and it must have been a bit of a nightmare for David and Philip. 'Argue, argue,' I'd say. 'Argue for every one'." Not that it did the brothers any harm. In 1961 David's astute financial brain earned him a well-merited place on the group board; this structure in Bristol lasted until 1966, when Philip Bollom became managing director, and David succeeded Tom Johnson as chairman of Bollom in 1969.

All was not plain sailing, however. At the end of 1964 Bollom had been advised that the Horfield Road factory would be subject to compulsory purchase by the Bristol Hospital Board, and it was quite a blow. The works were processing 23 tons of dry cleaning from 116 branches a week as well as two tons of dyeing, and the task of finding a suitable replacement would be no easy matter. There was a potential site near by, an old bakery in considerable disorder, but many of the largely elderly folk who lived around it did not take to the idea of a bustling revival of industry in the neighbourhood, and when they heard that a 95-foot chimney would be part of the new development they formed an action group to protest. After a long delay the Labour Housing Minister, Richard Crossman, took their side, so Bollom had to look elsewhere, much to the dismay of many loyal staff members who would find difficulty in travelling any great distance to work. This sense of something more than irritation was compounded when the maternity hospital built on the Horfield Road site turned out to have a chimney considerably taller than the one contemplated by Bollom.

But it was second time lucky. A larger and more modern building that would prove relatively easy to convert was found at Novers Hill, in Ivor Bollom's old Bedminster stamping ground. There was a ready source of labour in the little streets around, and in the two years between 1965 and 1967 work went ahead on creating one of the most advanced and automated dry cleaning plants in the world. When it was completed, 150 workers there could handle a turnover of £400,000 per year, compared with the £50,000's worth of cleaning handled by a similar number of Horfield Road personnel some 30 years earlier. At £250,000 the conversion was not a cheap exercise, but the combination of compensation for the loss of the old factory and the sale of some company assets made the bill quite manageable.

There were other problems to be faced in the late 1960s, and early in 1965 there was personal sadness for the Bollom brothers when their father Ivor died in Bournemouth at the age of 68. He had retired down to the South Coast, where he spent several happy years and kept up his interest in bowls. His brother Fred lived close by, and as Philip's twin sister Sheila had married a Bournemouth hotelier he did not want for family company. The funeral was on February 3 at Redland Park Congregational Church in Bristol, when the Rev. Basil Sims spoke of him in moving terms:

"Ivor Bollom, or Bert, as many called him, had a personality all his own which not only inspired his life of personal achievement but also inspired the lives of literally hundreds of people. His was a pioneer spirit, a questing zeal and a unique blending of artless enthusiasm and mature common sense. He lived his life passionately and vivaciously, yet always purposefully. To meet him was to meet a man who knew the secret of living; to talk with him was to find that he could share that secret with you; and then to leave his company was, and is for us now, to walk with head held high . . .

"There is no mystery, no hidden secret, in his success. He had a creative as well as a restless mind. Business problems were opportunities, challenges – not insurmountable obstacles, occasions for bewilderment or frustration. He himself, in Kipling's words, knew how to 'fill the unforgiving minute with 60 seconds' worth of distance run'. He worked with zest, with a clear mind and discerning insight; and by his enthusiasm, example and encouragement he drew the best out of his colleagues and associates and even helped them to develop similar characteristics. Always he had the human understanding, the human touch. Those who worked with him and for him honoured him as a man who understood their point of view, who was utterly honest, fearlessly frank and completely unselfish. There are many who knew him as a businessman. They will know that I reflect their feelings when I say publicly that they honoured him and that they loved him."

A month after Ivor Bollom's death the man who had been his first employee at Stokes Croft, Bill Jarrett, retired at the age of 60. By coincidence he had also moved to Bournemouth to be manager of the works there, and Philip Bollom travelled south to present him with his retirement gift. As he headed back for Bristol that evening he mused on the events of the past month, and the changing of the old order. And looking ahead, he knew the challenges facing his company, the group and the industry would call for managers with all the personal qualities enumerated by the Rev. Mr. Sims at Redland just a few weeks previously.

9 — Mr. Tom in the Chair

After being appointed group managing director in 1964 Tom Johnson succeeded Douglas Crockatt as chairman two years later – and he had scarcely sat down before the industry was facing its most pressing crisis since thc wartime bombs. By the autumn of 1966 Harold Wilson's Government had run into serious financial difficulties, and it was a situation in which one piece of bad news was followed by another infinitely worse. Unemployment was rising, inflation was on an upward curve and with wages being held back, that figure of an annual 10 per cent increase in demand for cleaning was nothing more than a happy memory. The figure for the years from 1966 to 1970 was nearer 2½ per cent, but any hope of coping with this problem without major distress was dashed by the introduction of Selective Employment Tax. The stated aim of SET was to shift labour, one of the factors of production, away from service industries into the ailing manufacturing sector. Dry cleaning is a service industry, albeit one that was deemed to be vital to the country's wellbeing during war time, and the combination of heavy penalties and investment allowance cuts placed upon it savaged the profitability of the group almost overnight. Tom Johnson recalls annual group profits being slashed by £500,000; his son Sands, who was with John Crockatt in Leeds at that time, remembers looking at the company's accounts for the summer quarter of 1968 and thinking "these look good". By the end of the year all profit had disappeared.

This time Tom Johnson found himself spearheading a reorganisation far more far-reaching than the rationalisation of the early 1960s. Large numbers of shops were closed, along with several factories on which large sums had been spent in modernisation, and the chairman was not the only director to be distressed by the resultant redundancies. Shops that showed low profits were closed and leased to produce profitable rents. Unit shops with on-the-spot cleaning facilities became increasingly the norm in place of labour-intensive works, and in the Bollom area alone the factories at Bournemouth and Cardiff went under; so, in the end, did the one at Plymouth opened with such high hopes at the start of the decade. One option closed to the group was that of raising costs to the customer; times, after all, were tight for them, too. In 1967 the question became academic since the Government imposed a prices freeze and besides, competition in the high street was as fierce as ever. "In the area covered by Bollom-shops alone there were three substantial competitors in Brooks, Quality and Welsh Cleaners, while innumerable small firms controlled nearly half the market. Price rises would always have been risky, even without all the other considerations," Philip Bollom recalls.

David Bollom was proving a valuable director in Bootle with his firm grasp of commerce and finance, but in 1971 he took the entire board by surprise, not to mention many others who thought they knew him well, by announcing that he planned to resign his post to apply for ordination in the Church of England. His interest in church matters, and indeed that of his brother, had been well known, but none had suspected that his commitment ran so deep. He succeeded in his aim, however, and Canon Bollom is now an incumbent in Surrey, far removed from his original calling. The vacancy created on the board by his departure was filled in 1972 by his brother Philip, who in the following year spearheaded a potentially advantageous but difficult Bollom reorganisation after the purchase of Welsh Dry Cleaners, with its 40 branches and modern plant at Treforest. The decision was made to close all the company's remaining receiving shops along with the Novers Hill factory in Bristol, and Treforest became the centre for the company's ever more significant textile rental operation.

By this stage the worst of the difficulties faced in Mr. Tom's early years in the chair had receded, and a combination of a sleeker, fitter dry cleaning service and progress in the towel hire and garment rental field gave him the happy task of reporting the most successful year in the company's history in 1972. It was a welcome and deserved return to good fortune for a man who had served the family firm well since his recruitment as a 5s.-a-week lab assistant at the age of 17 in 1927, only to take the reins nearly 40 years later at a time when the industry seemed to be falling down around his ears.

Like his father, Sir Ben's brother Sands, Tom Johnson studied dyeing and textiles in a non-degree course at Leeds University, all the time itching to return to Bootle and the real world. He did so in 1932, and for the next seven years he picked up wide-ranging management experience both at the works and out in the branches, with Sir Ben keeping an avuncular eye on his progress until his death in 1937. By now he was already "Mr. Tom", in that time-honoured way that family firms have of distinguishing between various managerial members, but in 1939 he was more than prepared to exchange this cosy tag for a plain number and rank, volunteering for the Royal Artillery as soon as war broke out. He was selected as an officer serving in North Africa, the Middle East and Italy, where he was mentioned in despatches and wounded in action in 1943. Now a captain, he was posted to the Royal Army Ordnance Corps when he was fit again, returning to Italy to be stationed in Naples. By this time word had got through to the top brass that Captain Johnson was a dyer and cleaner in civvy street, and for the rest of the war he found himself taking over all the dyehouses in Southern Italy to colour British khaki battledresses bright green for Italian prisoners of war. "Half a million of them," he swears, "and that's how Sands and Michael's dad won the war." He must have done something right in those dyehouses, however, for he held the rank of major when he was demobilised to return to his intensely busy but blitz-stricken family business in 1945.

He was appointed a director in his absence in 1940, when such matters must have seemed very removed from his life, and when he returned he became assistant to Oswald Gunnell, who was both chairman and managing director. His chief preoccupation in these early years was with the reorganisation of Mildmay Road to cope with the public's seemingly insatiable demand for cleaning. And then, as we have noted earlier, when he became managing director of Johnson Brothers on Mr. Gunnell's retirement in 1952, several years of his career were dominated by the rationalisation of the group's transport policy, and the widespread transfer of branches that came with it. It was painstaking, detailed and not always pleasant work, taking him the length of the country, but it at least helped to prepare him for some of the traumas lurking round the corner in the next decade. By the time he became group managing director in 1964 the changeover to unit shops was at its peak, an expensive and stressful time. And then, after Douglas Crockatt's retirement, came his elevation to group chairmanship in 1966 – and the hammer blow of Selective Employment Tax. There had also been two takeover threats to be staved off, niggling precursors of the even more bitter struggles that were to bedevil his successor John Crockatt in the late 1970s and early 1980s, and in each case the prospective buyer had been attracted by the company's huge portfolio of high street

Top: horse-riding was one of the enjoyments of Philip Bollom's youth. He is seen here on *Emerald Isle* at his family home at Broadlands, Long Ashton, near Bristol in the 1940s.

Bottom: the fulfilment of a dream, the opening of the rebuilt Broadmead Baptist Church in central Bristol in October 1969. Philip Bollom, as chairman of the church trustees and the Broadmead Building Trust, addresses a gathering that includes the Archdeacon of Bristol, the Rev. W. J. Grant, the president of the Baptist Union, architect Mr. Ronald Sims and Broadmead's minister, the Rev, J. Penry Davies.

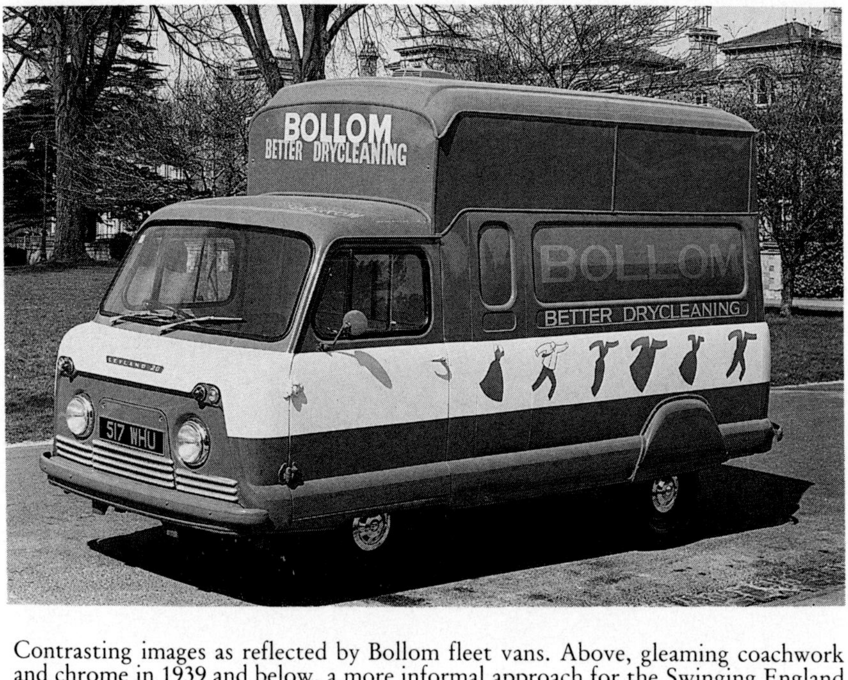

Contrasting images as reflected by Bollom fleet vans. Above, gleaming coachwork and chrome in 1939 and below, a more informal approach for the Swinging England of 1964.

Above, Philip and David Bollom with their father shortly before their family firm joined the Johnson Group in 1955. And below, the brothers in conference with Tom Johnson, who became chairman of the newly acquired company.

A last group portrait of the Bollom board in March 1955. From left to right are P. Bollom, F. P. Radford, S.J., I.B., F.A. and D. Bollom, and C. R. Williams.

Tom Johnson with his wife Nancy and two of Philip Bollom's cousins who served the company well, John Bollom, general manager for Wales, and Donald Brooks, works manager at Horfield Road.

properties, built up over several decades. "The first, in 1953, was a Colonel Brighten," Tom Johnson recalls. "He was very active at that time, and it all began when he wrote to Douglas Crockatt, who had not long been in the chair, saying that he wanted to buy the group. This was in about the May, and Douglas Crockatt replied to the effect that as the holiday season was approaching, he would not be able to make a formal reply until September. All that summer we beavered away, changing the structure of the group and tucking all our properties away in a separate company – and by the time September came around the new package was no longer one that held any attractions for Colonel Brighten. The next approach was in the 1960s, during my early years of chairmanship. From the mid-60s onwards we were aware that we had attracted the attention of that well-known man about the City of that time, Oliver Jessel. He was buying shares as fast as he could lay his hands on them through eight nominees, and we would watch each month how their holdings had grown until they topped the three million mark. Then, at last, in 1968, he wrote to say that he wanted to see me. I met him with Arthur Winspear, who later joined the group board, but who at that time was the director of the merchant bankers S. G. Warburg with special responsibility for Johnson affairs. Mr. Jessel said he wanted a place on the board. I said I didn't want him to. He said that if he got 51 per cent of the shares it wouldn't matter whether I wanted him to or not, and while there was no denying that, the fact remained that it was a hypothetical statement. I'm happy to say it remained hypothetical. A few months later he was in financial difficulties and he sold the lot of our shares.

"He was a threat for three years, three years in which I was constantly looking over my shoulder. It puts such unreasonable strain on a management, this pressure from behind, and you run the constant risk of making decisions for all the wrong reasons. You make sure you keep in with your institutional backers, of course, and keep them abreast of the situation, but it's a time-consuming business. It's just the price you pay for a free market economy, I suppose." Those battles were still on Tom Johnson's mind when he addressed workers at his retirement presentation in 1975. He told them of the approaches, and added: "On each occasion I felt that if we sold to the bidder he would probably have closed down the dry cleaning side and concentrated on the property interests. I was appalled that six thousand people might be put out of work because of me. We fought off the bids, and we won – so contrary to general belief that you have been working for me, it has rather been that I have been working for you." Long before that retirement speech, however, when the good times had started to roll again there was not a Johnson employee who had not been happy for Mr. Tom.

Outside work he has followed the example of Sir Ben, Douglas Crockatt and other Johnson executives by taking an active and valuable part in community life. He has served on hospital boards, on MENCAP locally and on the committee of Liverpool and Birkenhead Workshops for the Blind. He has been chairman of the Merseyside branch of the Institute of Directors and a member of its national council, and has been a director of the Liverpool Post and Echo and of Norwich Union Insurance locally; he is also a past chairman of South Sefton magistrates, and of the Sefton Council for Voluntary Services. Nationally, Tom Johnson has played a leading part in dry cleaning and dyeing trade association affairs, particularly in the foundation of the Association of British Launderers and Cleaners, an amalgamation of two separate bodies. And golf, the great sporting love of his life, led him twice to the captaincy of the West Lancashire Golf Club, the second time in its centenary year, and to a reputation as an after-dinner speaker which finally forced him to ration his appearances. He still has the scripts of all those addresses, and those who heard him regularly swear that he never repeated a joke or anecdote. There was an avalanche of warmth and goodwill for Tom Johnson – and for the devoted wife who in 1934 sentenced herself to a lifetime of being known as "Mrs. Tom" – at various gatherings of workers and directors when he, in his phrase, "hung up his dyehouse clogs" in 1975. "The boss has been a man who cares," director David Fowler told some 365 workers who congregated from all over the country to see what he had bought with the money they had collected for him. And there were roars of laughter from those who knew the side of him that had urged the Bollom brothers to beat down the landlords' rent when he displayed his new hi-fi equipment with the resounding words: "I got it at the old price".

10 — New Names, New Ventures

John Crockatt's ten years of chairmanship from 1975 to 1985 saw the group expand through both acquisition and natural growth, and the textile rental side of the business take off in quite spectacular style. This period also brought a series of irksome takeover battles and, more positively, an exciting and continuing drive into the United States market. Both of these topics will be treated more fully in later chapters.

John Lethem, Douglas Crockatt's elder son, was 26 when he joined Pullars of Perth in 1946 after serving as a Merchant Navy officer during the war. By this time his father was a well-established figure on the group board, 50 years old and looking forward to the day Oswald Gunnell would relinquish the chair to him; but the Crockatt family's connections with the famous old Scottish dyers stretched back far beyond Johnson's acquisition of the firm in 1938, for in the early years of the last century their forbear Peter Campbell had married a Pullar widow. It was thus with particular interest that John Crockatt took up his new appointment.

As the years progressed he took on increasing responsibility at Pullars, rising to the post of managing director in 1959. A year later he transferred to Bootle to take on the same role with Johnson Brothers, at the same time gaining a place on the group board, and in 1972 he was appointed managing director of the Johnson Group and the chairman of Crockatt in Leeds and several other group companies. Three years later he succeeded Tom Johnson as chairman.

His years brought a decade of continuous growth which produced some impressive statistics. In 1974, the last full year before his rise to the top, group turnover was £11.6 millions, with pre-tax profit at £1.1 million. By 1984 turnover was up to £70.2 millions, showing a profit of £6.6 millions, and in the same ten years unit shop sales rose from £9 millions to £38 millions. He saw the number of unit shops rise from 550 to 691, with numerous minor acquisitions and the friendly takeover of Zernys in the Hull area in 1977, Kneels in the South-west in 1978 and Hayes in the London region in the following year. The latter two were particularly strong in textile rental – by buying Hayes, in fact, the group completed its national coverage in this field – and this contributed to another set of impressive figures. In 1974, turnover from the textile rental operation stood at £580,000; in 1984 the figure was £17 millions, paving the way to an even more substantial presence in the market since then.

Away from the office John Crockatt has maintained a lifelong interest in boats and yachting and is a qualified light aircraft pilot. He loved climbing as a young man, and while it is sometimes surprising to Sassenachs to learn that the game of cricket flourishes north of the border, he looks back happily to playing for Perthshire C.C.C. His time at Pullars also saw him made a High Constable of Perth, as well as holding office in the community's chamber of commerce and Rotary Club, and he was an active council member of the Scottish Association of Dyers and Cleaners. Down south in Liverpool – he now lives in retirement with his wife Jo close to the sand dunes and red squirrels of Formby Point – he was prominent on both the Merseyside and Bootle chambers of commerce, became a justice of the peace and found time amid the trials and takeover bids of his chairmanship to study law and gain his Bachelor's Degree in 1976. On reflection, his long hours of preparing documents for the Office of Fair Trading, institutions and shareholders probably taught him more about company law in action than any number of textbooks and lectures. Like some chairmen before him, including his father, he has taken an active interest in a financial institution by becoming a director of the Universities Superannuation Scheme, Britain's seventh-largest pension fund, in 1984, and another honour he shared with his father was his term as Prime Warden of the Dyers' Company in 1980–81, fifteen years after Mr. Douglas had held the post. He also rose high in the Varsity International Conference of Cleaners, the unusual trade association that did so much to build up the group's contacts and confidence in the United States.

"Everything he touches he does well," Philip Bollom said of John Crockatt when he retired. "This characteristic is one that has served the group in such good stead during his long career. His comprehensive outlook has enabled John to see both great and small matters in true perspective, and this clear sense of purpose, his courage, his zeal and his wisdom have had an incalculable influence on the Johnson Group." The incoming chairman praised his predecessor's resolution, skill and determination in the face of a succession of hostile takeover bids – "It was his leadership that made sure of our survival" – and he listed his other qualities as the ability to bring people together and motivate them, to identify and achieve goals, to communicate his ideas and to earn respect for his clear decision-making ability and high personal integrity.

While the Johnson Group's Transatlantic ventures will warrant a chapter of their own, one aspect of the American Connection had a profound effect on U.K. operations – the transformation of textile rental from an interesting sideline to an increasingly influential section of the business, and one with exciting growth potential. Johnson has the largest share of Britain's dry cleaning market, with 25 per cent-plus, but it is still only number four in the rental field with a six per cent market share – a happy enough position, but one that leaves it with plenty of future targets. It all started during Tom Johnson's time in the chair with a cabinet towel hire service in 1970 which spread to all its operating companies over the ensuing two years. The breakthrough came, however, through John Crockatt's links with the Varsity International Conference – and more specifically, through the success of an Ohio-based member of the conference, Bill Pulley, in franchising a rental system to growing numbers of American dry cleaners. In 1970 Pulley and two other cleaners, spurred by a recession every bit as painful as the one afflicting the industry in Britain, sat round a table together to discuss ways in which they could diversify. They gathered facts and figures that suggested that the hire and regular cleaning and replacement of uniforms and overalls had potential – but it was a complicated business, and one full of pitfalls for the small independent dry cleaners who formed the overwhelming part of the American market. This was a boom time for franchises in the United States, with fast food operations like Kentucky Fried Chicken grabbing the headlines with sensational trading figures, and Pulley and his colleagues called in a management consultant and an expert in production and space utilisation to see whether they could draw up a marketable formula that would open the textile rental door to all efficient retail cleaners. Each founder tested the system for a year in his own business and found that it worked, and in May 1971 Apparelmaster Inc. was launched.

The Johnson Group broke new ground when it became Apparelmaster's exclusive licensee in Britain in January 1974. By 1976 it was the corporation's largest franchise holder, with ten central works converted to garment rental servicing, and as we have noted earlier, the purchase of Kneels and James Hayes completed its national coverage in this field by 1979. Before this, in 1975, the group accepted the offer of a 17.5 per cent shareholding in Apparelmaster Inc., and John Crockatt was asked to go on the American company's board; the newly-elected Conservative Government lifted currency controls in 1979 and by 1981, with the founders anxious to realise some capital out of their venture, the Johnson Group snapped up the opportunity to buy a controlling interest in the firm and make it a wholly owned subsidiary. Today Apparelmaster franchises can be found not only in the United States and Britain but in Canada, Australia and New Zealand. They all benefit from a package that transcends operating and marketing procedures to include such specialised services as field consultant visits, tele-conferences, training schools, workshops and plant tours. Members are also kept fully in touch with new rental opportunities, which have long outstripped simple towel and garment hire to take in warm air driers and soap dispensers for washrooms, bed and table linen, dust-mats bearing company logos if required, replaceable mopheads and industrial wiping cloths in high-absorbing cotton.

In workwear rental items are personalised, with each wearer usually allotted three garments – one in use, one being cleaned and the third in reserve. Whether through sociological reasons or simply because of climatic differences, Americans tend to change their overalls three times as often as their British counterparts, for whom once a week seems quite enough. This, combined with the fact that only about a third of the nine million British workers who wear overalls are at present covered by rental services, prompts Johnson to believe that there is scope for expansion for years to come. Company policy is to educate customers into changing their clothes more often and to gain fresh business by fast and reliable service and a wide choice of well-made, comfortable and stylish garments. It is expected that increasing numbers of these will be manufactured at Apparelmaster Design Ltd., a company near Wigan whose story will be told more fully in the chapter on Philip Bollom's years as chairman. In all these operations the group contracts to rent out the items with the undertaking to clean and distribute them regularly, and its policy of operating from local works within daily van range of its customers makes it a fully national textile rental service operator in the U.K., in spite of its relatively low share of the market. It also boasts a prestigious and highly specialised subsidiary in Johnson Micronclean, based in Perth, which incorporates the most advanced technology in decontamination methods. It supplies and services the special protective clothing required for cleanroom operations in micro-electronic industries, pharmaceutical manufacture, medicine and increasingly in the food industry.

Many of these developments stemmed from John Crockatt's years as chairman, and they have been capitalised on since. But when Mr. Crockatt looks back on his decade at the top today, he is also conscious of what at the time must have seemed an almost ceaseless intrusion into his positive work for the company – the great takeover battles of the late 1970s and early '80s.

11 — The Price of a Free Market

Attempts to buy control of the Johnson Group had not been unknown in the past, as we have noted. Douglas Crockatt kept Colonel Brighten waiting in vain through that damp Coronation summer of 1953, and later came Tom Johnson's icily polite luncheon with Oliver Jessel. The first of a series of even greater threats, however, came in the late 1970s, when a bid was made by Sketchley, the competitors along with whom the Johnson Group dominates the dry cleaning market. Two very different companies – Sketchley is a centralised organisation with a national name, though it remains strongest in its traditional southern heartland – the rivals each enjoyed a share of the market of about 23 per cent. As the Monopolies and Mergers Commission is always likely to look into any takeover that pushes a company much above a 25 per cent market share the Sketchley approach baffled many Johnson executives at the time, and they remain convinced to this day that the bidders had been given woefully poor advice. Relations between the two great rivals had always been placid enough – "you could say we were on good terms with them, at arm's length," says John Crockatt, the chairman of the day – but after the brothers who had built Sketchley up had retired, a new management with fresh ideas moved in. The first John Crockatt knew of their interest was when a letter was hand-delivered to Bootle warning him that a bid was to be made. His initial move was to phone the group's merchant bankers, Warburg and Co., and that is how Arthur Winspear became a central figure in Johnson's defence against the Sketchley bid – which rose to an offer price of 42p. per share – and indeed in subsequent ones. "He's so able," says John Crockatt. "He must be one of the best bid-fighters the country has ever seen."

Mr. Crockatt certainly saw enough of Arthur Winspear to form this view, as for the next three months his life and that of his brother Allan, by this time group deputy chairman, revolved around Warburg's London offices in Gresham Street. The first move was for each company to make submissions to the Office of Fair Trading, which was soon persuaded, perhaps not surprisingly, that this was a case for the Monopolies and Mergers Commission to examine. "In nine cases out of ten that would have been the end of it," says John Crockatt. "But this, of course, was the tenth case. Sketchley said they'd fight it. For three weeks we worked like mad to prepare a case, mustering all the facts, figures and even hearsay evidence we could find. It was expensive and it was appallingly time-consuming. Then, after all that, Sketchley pulled out. We were relieved, of course, and glad that it was over, but it was a frustrating and harassing time."

The next spate of harassment and frustration was not long in coming, for in the summer of 1982 came a further unwelcome approach. This time the bidder was Sunlight, a company half the size of the Johnson Group with scant experience of dry cleaning. Again its management was young and expansionist-minded, and John Crockatt and Philip Bollom met them in a London hotel to listen to "the usual spiel". John Crockatt told them that he would report back on the board's decision the following morning, and the answer was inevitably no. It was again a case for the Office of Fair Trading, they again passed it on to the Monopolies and Mergers Commission – and then a complicating factor reared its head. Initial Services, giants in the textile rental business, decided to come in on the back of the Sunlight bid of 278p. per share and state their own intention to make an offer, after being rebuffed in a half-hearted approach a year previously. As it turned out they never made a formal bid, but nevertheless the Monopolies and Mergers Commission found themselves with two approaches for Johnson to consider – and their report that both would be against the public interest came only after six months' hard labour by Arthur Winspear, senior group executives and a number of outside experts, all at a time when the venture into the United States was gaining momentum and should have been the dominant issue. Indeed, it has been estimated that the dual bids held up the expansion programme into the U.S.A. by almost a year, though many would say that time has been more than made up since then. Be that as it may, back in 1982, as yet another judgement went in its favour, there were the occasional dark mutterings among rivals that the Johnson Group was sheltering behind the skirts of the Monopolies and Mergers Commission – a totally spurious argument, since that clinically impartial body is concerned only with what it sees as the public good, rather than the susceptibilities of company directors, workers and shareholders in Bootle or any other part of the world. So it was with a certain sense of grim satisfaction that the group found itself forced to repel the last hostile bid of the early 1980s, in September 1984, with all the resolution and persuasion it could muster; for this was an argument that went all the way to the shareholders.

The bidders were the Nottingham Manufacturing Company, a successful Midlands-based organisation which supplied a significant part of its output in textiles and hosiery to Marks and Spencer, who at that time had spent some years pursuing a high-profile "Buy British" campaign. In the Johnson Group's submission to the Office of Fair Trading it was suggested that M. & S. were retreating from this policy and this, together with a decline in the British textile industry generally, put Nottingham in a vulnerable position. John Crockatt's first knowledge of the bid came when N.M.C.'s chairman, Mr. Harry Djanogly, approached him and suggested that as his company made clothes, and the Johnson Group cleaned them, it was only natural that they should join together. Mr. Crockatt confessed that the equation had never struck him before. More important, he got on the phone to Warburg and Co. to pick the brains of the merchant banker who succeeded Arthur Winspear in specialising in the group's affairs, Stephen Latner. By this time Mr. Winspear was a Johnson director, and John Crockatt describes his reappearance in the fray to fight the Nottingham bid after serious heart surgery as "one of the most astonishing and moving moments in my business experience."

The submission put together by the Johnson Group to go before the Office of Fair Trading is a classic of its *genre*, full of critical comment and innuendo against N.M.C. and its chairman that must rank as a masterpiece of non-libellous abuse. It stresses what Johnson saw as Nottingham's trading weakness, quotes press reports that described Mr. Djanogly as autocratic and inaccessible to brokers, analysts and journalists, and adds the only slightly expurgated views of various contacts in the Midlands. Everyone concerned with fighting hostile takeovers admits that it is a rough, tough business, with no quarter asked or given. Mr. Djanogly, of course, was not inactive at this time, either; exactly what he told the Office of Fair Trading about his impressions of the Johnson Group is not to hand, but all that mattered to him, at the end of the day, was the fact that the O.F.T. shared his view that this was indeed not a case to be referred to the Monopolies and Mergers Commission.

Thus it was that for the first time, the battle was taken to the shareholders. "Say NO to Nottingham's totally unacceptable bid" was the group's uncompromising message to them, telling them of the exciting new possibilities of trading in the United States, a forecast of record profits of £7.1 millions by June 1985, and the prospect of record dividends of 18.6p. per share for 1984 – "if Nottingham's bid fails". Perhaps of even greater importance, in the final week of the battle John Crockatt, the then group deputy managing director Terry Greer and Jim Wahl of the American Johnson Group Inc. took their "road show" out and about, urging the investment managers of the big institutional shareholders that they should stay with the company rather than accept Nottingham's cash bid of 440p. per share. In the event Nottingham acquired 9 per cent of Johnson Group shares, but since that time the Djanogly family has sold the company to Coats Viyella, and the Johnson stock has been divided among a number of major institutions.

John Crockatt, who retired with several projects left unfinished as a result of fighting the bids, shares Tom Johnson's view that this kind of unwarranted intrusion into a company's resources is the price paid for a free market economy. "There was such a lot of personal abuse involved in takeover bids in those days," he recalls.

If there was one man who revelled in such situations, however, it was Arthur Winspear, with his sharp tongue to repel all boarders and mastery of press, communications and the art of mustering public opinion. It was his good fortune that the Johnson headquarters are in unemployment-bedevilled Liverpool, where any threat to jobs would always bring out the best in the likes of Eric Heffer, Bootle's socialist M.P., and Crosby's Shirley Williams, neither of whom might normally be expected to share too much common ground with a City merchant banker. The press announcement by the bidder; Johnson's instant and astringent riposte and then, if it came to it, the offer document and the one put out by the board to fight it off. All were meat and drink to the man John Crockatt sees as a bid-fighter to go down in history, and who to Philip Bollom is simply "our incomparable Arthur Winspear".

12 — West to America

In the field of dry cleaning in the United Kingdom, the Johnson Group's 25 per cent-plus share of the market means that any major acquisition would be certain to attract the attention of the Monopolies and Mergers Commission. That is why the textile rental sector, of which the group has a modest 6 per cent share, will be increasingly important in the years ahead - as will the exciting growth in the United States. When it is considered that the U.K. textile rental operation has its origins in Cincinnati with Apparelmaster, the purchase of which is told more fully in Chapter 10, the transatlantic influence on the group's finances cannot be stressed too strongly.

All this is very recent history - yet contact with the United States, where marketing techniques have always been to the fore, stretches back to a visit by Tom Johnson's father Mr. Sands in 1905. Oswald Gunnell, Tom Johnson and his son Sands and Douglas Crockatt all followed in his footsteps, and after Sands Johnson's four-month stay in the late 1950s study visits by directors became a regular feature of life. The breakthrough came in 1967, when the group joined the Varsity International Conference of Cleaners, thanks chiefly to John Crockatt's being in the right place at the right time twelve months earlier. A British member firm had just dropped out, and when Mr. Crockatt met two leading lights in Varsity while on a visit to the U.S. in October 1966 it was not long before invitations were extended.

Varsity is an unusual institution, perhaps unique even in highly-motivated America. It can best be described as a competitive seminar. Every October a maximum of 20 member companies - there strictly by invitation - meet for a wide ranging discussion on the state of the industry and for the exchange of ideas and information, and each day they award the other participants marks for the quality of their performance. At the end of the week the bottom two or three firms lose their membership, and others are invited to take their place the following autumn. "It involves a lot of preparatory work, putting together a binder of all the good things you've done in the previous twelve months," says John Crockatt. "Then, once you are there, the programme is very hard-working, swift-moving and highly planned. When the Johnson Group left Varsity in 1984 we were the only non-U.S. members. In the past there had been member companies from Switzerland and Holland, as well as Australia and Canada, but if English was not your first language you were always likely to struggle in the fast-talking meetings, however impressive your firm's achievements had been."

Varsity was founded towards the end of the last war, when a director of an American cleaning and dyeing trade journal set about rebuilding contacts broken by the hostilities by inviting major companies to meet to exchange ideas to help advance the industry. "Varsity" has fewer university connotations than in Britain, and can simply mean the first team, the pick of the bunch, and that is how member companies have continued to see themselves. After Johnson's first meeting in 1967 John Crockatt continued to visit Varsity almost annually throughout his term in the chair, and indeed keeps up contact with it in retirement. But in 1984, with its American expansion taking off in a big way, the group found it no longer tenable to remain in a forum in which complete frankness and openness of information are bywords; an essential feature of Varsity is the fact that while all member companies are rivals around the conference table, they are not in active competition out in the shopping malls. The way Johnson was taking off in the United States, it was no longer possible to know that this autumn's Varsity colleagues would not be next spring's competitors in the battle for the dry cleaning dollar out there in some Mid-Western town.

The group's years of membership of Varsity proved invaluable, giving senior executives a vital insiders' view of the idiosyncracies of the vast American market. Even more important were the contacts made, the first and crucial one being Bill Pulley of Apparelmaster. To recap briefly, Johnson became the Cincinnati-based textile rental franchise company's sole British licensees early in 1974, acquired a 17.5 per cent holding in 1975 and a controlling interest in 1981; the remaining minority was acquired in 1982. Apparelmaster, headed by the highly competent Liz Remle, now licenses garment rental systems to some 300 franchisees in the United States, Britain, Canada, Australia and New Zealand.

Johnson Group Inc. was set up as a wholly-owned United States holding company in October 1981, and from then on the American expansion took off rapidly, checked only by the British takeover battles of the early 1980s. The first shops chain to be acquired was Tuchman Cleaners Inc., now with some 28 outlets in greater Indianapolis, who came into the Johnson fold in February 1982. For a New World business its roots run deep, for it was founded in the early years of this century by Sam Tuchman, a young Jewish immigrant from Poland who headed westward to open a tailor's shop in Indiana after finding his feet in America in New York. Here his story parallels that of Ivor Bollom back in the Old World in Bristol, for it was the depression and a falling-away of orders for new clothes that prompted him to look to wholesale dry cleaning as an additional source of income, and his son Sid was just ten years old when he started helping out with the business. It must be confessed that not all his thoughts were on it in his early years, for he took off for Hollywood as a young man to try his luck in films. Like many a hopeful before and since, however, it was not long before he was back in the old home town, and from then until his retirement from the Johnson Group Inc. board in December 1987 he devoted his working life to the dry cleaning industry. He first became known to Johnson executives as a member of the Apparelmaster board in the 1970s, and quickly impressed them with his gifts as a lucid and articulate communicator. He has twice visited Britain to deliver textile rental seminars, and each time he proved a big hit with his entertaining, informal and positive style. That time in Hollywood was obviously not altogether wasted!

Sid joined the J.G.I. board in 1982 and soon proved a thought-provoking and challenging member, sometimes provocative, always effective and never averse to questioning accepted wisdom. His deep knowledge of the cleaning and textile rental business and his lively approach to marketing and selling techniques assured him a ready audience among his fellow directors, and it was typical of him that when he retired he chose to pursue his lifelong interest in teaching, speaking and management consultancy through a new venture, Tuchman Training Systems Inc. He soon became convinced of the wisdom of Tuchman Cleaners' move to the Johnson Group when he saw its garment rental service treble its turnover before his retirement, and towards the end of 1985 the company's main processing plant was completely renovated, with the result that 1986 profits were 40 per cent up on the 1985 figures. Jim Dunn, a creative and astute executive, is proving a highly competent successor to Sid Tuchman. And on a personal note, Sid and his wife Charlene provided Philip and Sheila Bollom with one of the finest of their many memories of America when they invited them to their daughter Ellen's wedding at the synagogue in Indianapolis.

Capitol Varsity of Ohio was the next transatlantic acquisition, in September 1983 – and this brought the Varsity Conference's Bill Pulley under the Johnson banner. The company, one of the most highly regarded in the United States, operates some 17 cleaning outlets and serves Dayton and Cincinnati with Apparelmaster garment rental; it was, of course, one of the three that pioneered and fine-tuned the Apparelmaster formula back in the early 1970s, so it can add an important place in the industry's history in America to its lengthy list of achievements. It came to the Johnson Group some years after a legal test case that had altered its profile as a company almost beyond recognition. From its foundation in 1924 to 1973 it was primarily a central plant operation based in Oxford, Ohio, and at one time it serviced more than 150 franchise stores in south-western Ohio and south-eastern Indiana. It had run a number of package plants since 1954, but by 1969 some seven-tenths of its revenue came from the central plant. All this was to change as a result of the inclusion of the dry cleaning industry in the U.S. Fair Labor Standards Act in 1968. This put the industry's wages and hours under the regulation of the Federal Government Labor Department, and it was not long before a number of dry cleaners sought to franchise their outlets as a means of escaping the restrictions of the Act. The Government needed a test case to establish a legal precedent for franchising, and since Capitol Varsity was the oldest such company in the industry it found itself under the microscope. The Labor Department filed suit against it, contending that its franchisees were employees rather than independent contractors, and the case struck at the heart of Capitol's strategy of selling dry cleaning through franchise stores. It resulted in the closure of the central plant and a loss of 70 per cent of the company's business overnight.

Bill Pulley set about rescuing what remained of his family business, reshaping it, upgrading its image through new marketing strategies and later moving or converting existing plants to drive-in or drive-through locations. The drive-through is now common in the United States, where relaxed planning laws allow small towns to sprawl out along the highways with neon-lit strips of petrol stations, fast-food restaurants, motels and businesses offering any number of services.

Very few such opportunities arise in this country, and if a suitable site becomes available it almost inevitably ends up as a petrol station. Of the handful of drive-ins or drive-throughs scattered around the Johnson Group on this side of the Atlantic, most involve an element of legwork on the customer's part; in America the whole transaction can often be carried out from the driving seat. One way and another, it seems likely that Britain will continue to lag behind in this field – but it was just what Bill Pulley was looking for in Ohio, and his restructured company has gone from strength to strength since then, not least in building up a high-speed shirt service in several of its shops. "Bill is a man of immense integrity and ability, determination and enterprise," says Philip Bollom. "He is a very highly regarded member of the J.G.I. board, with an independent outlook and strong opinions. I respect him greatly, as I do his wife Martha Lee, who majored in education at university and taught in Cincinnati at one time. Like me, she's a twin, so I always feel a certain affinity with her."

By the following spring, in April 1984, the group was welcoming Tom and Marguerite Garrett of Beaufort, South Carolina's Garrett Drycleaning Inc., previously the Three G Corporation. This is a business with 16 shops in Beaufort, Hilton Head Island and Savannah, Georgia, and one in which workwear rental plays an increasingly important role. Other Garrett shops, in Myrtle Beach and Charleston, have been taken over by Coleman Young Enterprises Inc. in a rationalisation that can only enhance the profitability of each company. Tom and Marguerite work closely together – Marguerite takes some delight in her nickname, among some people in the business, of "the steel magnolia" – and they form an important link in Johnson's impressively strong chain in South Carolina and Georgia. These sun belt states are developing rapidly, and it is not surprising that newcomers are flocking to gracious Savannah and its fine coastal surroundings. Tom is a keen sportsman who has won numerous awards for deep-sea fishing, and Philip and Sheila Bollom recall happy hours sailing with him and Marguerite along the beautiful and densely wooded coastline from Hilton Head Island to Beaufort.

Three months later came J. W. Enterprises of Wichita, now Best Cleaners Inc., who operate 30 dry cleaning shops and textile rental and laundry facilities around Wichita and Oklahoma City. The company's founder was John Woodhams, an astute businessman and

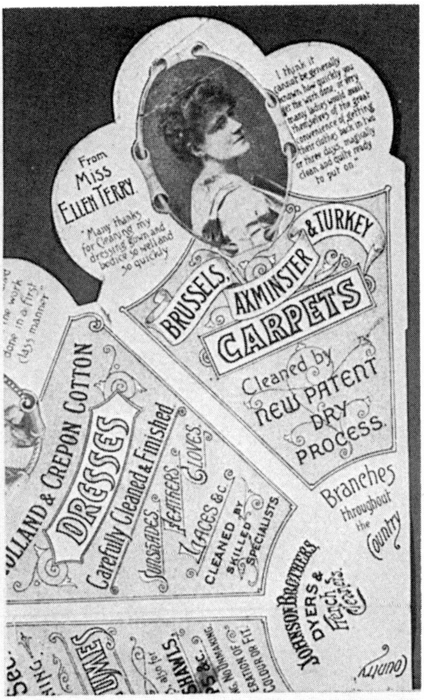

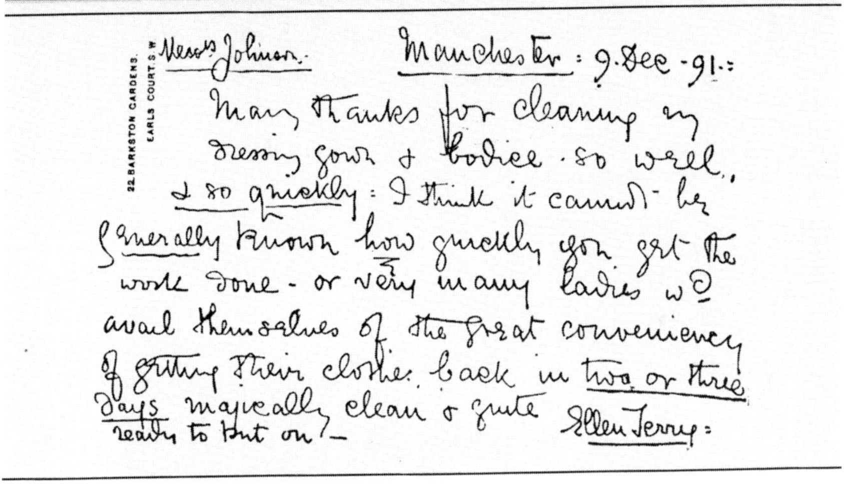
22 BARKSTON GARDENS. EARLS COURT. S.W.

Messrs Johnson. Manchester: 9. Dec -91.:

Many thanks for cleaning my dressing gown & bodice. so well, & so quickly: I think it cannot be generally known how quickly you get the work done - or very many ladies w^d avail themselves of the great convenience of getting their clothes back in two or three days magically clean & quite ready to put on —

Ellen Terry:

Johnson Brothers' advertising from the 1890s. It was a Victorian publicist's dream when the legendary Ellen Terry wrote to congratulate the firm on its services in 1891.

The first true Johnson group board in January 1921, shortly after the merger with Jas. Smith of Dewsbury and Flinn of Brighton. Standing: C. Cameron, H. P. Hadfield, Oswald Gunnell, C. A. Holt and Leonard Mitchell. Seated: Fred Johnson, Fred Flinn, John Smith, Sir Ben Johnson, T. Sands Johnson and W. E. Davies.

Lush and Cook's horse-drawn vans were a familiar sight in the streets of North London at the turn of the century.

Typical Johnson receiving branches of the past, taking up just half a shop floorspace. Right, Queen Street, Cardiff in Edwardian times, and below, at Herne Hill in 1937.

Left, Sir Ben Johnson in his later years, and below, in 1921, when he showed the Prince of Wales around the Bootle plant to the delight of hundreds of cheering workers.

Another royal occasion: Queen Mary visits the Eastman factory at The Vale, Acton, London in February 1927.

The morning after: bomb damage at Bootle in May 1941.

Another sorry scene from the 1941 bombing, looking south over the remains of the Bootle packing room.

ERRATUM Please note that the
captions for the photographs facing
page 65 ... with the photograph facing page 8...

sterling character, who built up a chain over a wide rural area spreading from the dusty Mexican border to the wheatfield states that roll into the Canadian prairies. At the time of the purchase there were some 50 stores trading under five different names, though all that remain have since acquired the Best Cleaners tag. Of more concern than the fragmented identity were disappointing sales, and in 1986 came a major reorganisation which brought a strengthening of the team and the sale of northern operations in Wisconsin and Minnesota. Some shops transferred to the capable hands of Bill Pulley and his team, and early in 1987 there was further streamlining when the southern shops around Albuquerque, New Mexico, were sold. Business is now very much concentrated in Wichita and Oklahoma City and Best is showing progress, especially since Jim Barry of the more recently acquired Pride Cleaners has taken it under his wing. This is another example of a company that has benefited from the kind of consolidation, rationalisation and cost-control available only to members of a larger group, and it will continue to do so even more in the years ahead.

On to September 1984, and an exciting acquisition in Al Phillips the Cleaner, with ten outlets in the unique city of Las Vegas, Nevada. Run by the flamboyant Shapiro brothers, Mel and Phil, these are high-turnover, high-profile shops which charge the top prices in town when they are not beating the drum about one of their out-of-this-world sales, and they are seen in the group and far beyond as masters of marketing. Not, of course, that such a formula would work in every location. "The Shapiros can lay out more on a sign than some of our companies spend on a whole shop," says J.G.I.'s president Jim Wahl. "They have to make a splash to compete with all the other glittering lights along the Las Vegas Strip, the emphasis is on huge drive-throughs, and it's all very up-beat. They know their area and they thrive in it, in spite of a sudden growth of competition in the Las Vegas market in recent times. They are typical examples of the strength of a group that leaves the business in the hands of local experts who know just what they have to do to earn results." One of their legendary signs, a running neon unit close to the M.G.M. Grand Hotel, cost $50,000, and the brothers say they will spend double that sum if the location is right: "We have more signage than any cleaners in the world, and it's been a worthwhile investment."

Looking back over more than two decades of success, Mel Shapiro puts it all down to presentation. "Every dry cleaner has the same machinery," he says. "We all have the same boilers and pressing equipment. Quality is taken for granted in any good operation. What can make you really successful, though, is effective marketing. You can have the best plant in the world, but if you don't know how to promote your services to the public it won't do you much good. Marketing has been our secret from the beginning." It is an approach that has carved out the company around 25 per cent of a massively competitive Las Vegas market, and it takes the form of snapping up the most visible and expensive sites for new stores, opening all night for this famously insomniac city, employing glamorous young women in hot pants to do the fetching and carrying – carhops, they call them – and flooding local television with prime-time commercials. They pulled off a coup back in the 1960s when they persuaded the likes of Sammy Davis Junior and Jimmy "Schnozzle" Durante to film TV endorsements for nothing more than some free dry cleaning. Since then they have tended to deliver their own scripts, a task made easier by the fact that Mel, the younger brother, was once a professional stand-up comedian. Sometimes they have been known to backfire. In one he and Phil were seen running to one of their shops in their underwear, trousers in hand, while a voice-over intoned "Drop your pants for Al Phillips!" Soon afterwards the pink-faced carhops were complaining that customers were driving up, unbuckling their rhinestone-studded belts and doing just that.

Phil started as a cleaner back in New York's Long Island in 1947, and it is generally accepted that he is the financial and technical brain, while Mel drums up the business on the Strip – and off it, for year-round business from local residents means more to them than the unreliable tourist market. Back in New York, Phil was one of the first cleaners to go into homes to remove curtains and replace them after cleaning. He also owned a successful store in Harlem, but in 1964 the brothers decided to follow the sun to Las Vegas and bought the first Al Phillips shop, next to the Sahara Hotel, from its namesake founder just seven months after it had opened. They liked the name well enough, saw no need to change it – and in two years they had one of the busiest over-the-counter plants in the States, charging the highest prices in town but offering unrivalled service in opening seven days a week until 11 p.m. In 1968 came their first 24-hour drive-through, which turned out same-day orders even on Sundays, and before long it was pulling in $27,000 a week.

With Al Phillips, however, there is always something more interesting to talk about than weekly turnover figures. Back in 1968 Frank Sinatra became a devoted customer when he found they were the only cleaners in town who could press a suit one Sunday afternoon. Henry Ford was in Vegas for a televised speech at noon one day when he realised, over breakfast, that his suit needed a clean. One might have imagined that Henry Ford would have had the foresight to pack a spare suit in his valise, or indeed could have sent out for a dozen new ones, but neither of these things apparently happened. He had someone call Al Phillips, and the offending garment was back to him by 11 a.m. When Sean Connery was filming the James Bond thriller *Diamonds Are Forever* in the late 1960s he allegedly had 40 identical beige suits and ties so that he would look immaculate in every take in this sticky desert town, and the Shapiros cleaned most of them every night. But perhaps the most lucrative showbiz order of all came when a roof in the wardrobe room of the Dunes Hotel collapsed, spraying all 800 fragile garments with dusty insulation material. They were all trucked back and forth to Al Phillips that night in time for the next performance, and no doubt the hotel management found the $14,000 cleaning bill the least of their problems. Unfortunately, not every star-studded story has a happy ending. The Shapiros found they were unable to help when Shirley MacLaine sent them a torn chiffon dress in the hope that it could be repaired. And Anthony Newley did an entire show at the Desert Inn in old blue jeans after his four tuxedos had been delayed on their journey from the cleaners to the hotel. "There's a tremendous amount of service required to keep celebrities and show people as your customers," says Phil Shapiro. "In many cases we can't make money on expensive clothes, but we do sometimes get some publicity out of it, and that often makes it worthwhile." The brothers certainly cannot be accused of having stardust in their eyes, in spite of their glamorous surroundings. "They have probably the most closely hands-on management I've ever seen," says Jim Wahl. "When production at one plant gets overburdened, they will transport the cleaning to another one and pick up the slack there. They perceive themselves as being exceptional, and consequently they are perceived that way in the community." Philip Bollom's view of the Shapiros is equally enthusiastic. "They are imaginative individualists who bubble with wit and good humour," he says. "Both Phil and Mel have great ability, and manage the unique business they have developed so successfully with exemplary skill and superb style."

It came as a major surprise to many people in Las Vegas and the wider American cleaning industry when the Shapiros, such noted free spirits, sold Al Phillips to the Johnson Group from far-away Cincinnati and even farther-away Great Britain at a time when their annual revenues were approaching $5 millions. "They made us the right offer at the right time," says Phil. "It's been business as usual, and Johnson has given us great autonomy." Phil is married to Trish, who has a showbiz background, while Mel's wife Florence is the daughter of the legendary "Miss Bluebell", Margaret Kelly. In January 1986 the couple visited the Bootle works with Ms. Kelly, who was in Britain to launch the BBC TV series on her career, and there was much entertaining banter about her early years on Merseyside.

As if to prove its local horses for local courses philosophy, Johnson's next move into the U.S. market, in January 1985, was for Coleman Young Enterprises Inc., trading as Quick as a Wink. With 50-plus shops through rural mid-state South Carolina, the company cannot match Al Phillips for turnover per unit or prices charged to the customer – yet on the other side of the coin, Al Phillips cannot match Quick as a Wink for low overheads and so, in their very different ways, both pull their full weight in contributing to group profits. For companies wishing to learn the lesson of the advantages of local management over a centralised bureaucracy, a comparative study of Al Phillips the Cleaner and Quick as a Wink tells the whole story.There are certainly not too many demands to clean Frank Sinatra's suits down in Spartanburg, S.C. One of Quick as a Wink's more pressing problems in recent years was a drought in 1986 which left the local farming community with more on their minds than having their suits cleaned, but good customer relations helped pull Coleman Young and his team through, with his big new drive-ins working especially well. Jim Wahl has particular admiration for the firm's management structure, ranging from the top down through three area managers, each of whom has four supervisors reporting to him. These supervisors are each responsible for four stores, and they also act as relief managers. On his home patch Coleman Young was a dedicated, hard-working professional with a knack of getting things done and a way of inspiring respect and admiration among colleagues and his workers. And as a member of the J.G.I. board he was always thoughtful and sound. "He is very much an achiever who founded and developed one of our largest and most successful American companies. He spoke when he had something positive to say – and then we all sat up and listened," says Philip Bollom. When the business was acquired, Coleman's talented son Cole Junior was appointed its president, with his father on the J.G.I. board. And when Coleman retired it was Cole who took his place on the board, in March 1989. Their wives Julia and Jenny share their staunch and active involvement in the Southern Baptist Church, and another of Philip Bollom's happy memories of the United States is of a Sunday morning service in Greenville, with 1,500 people packed in a superb modern building, the choir in full voice and the minister speaking with the kind of imagery and power that would have captivated Ivor Bollom half a century earlier.

December 1986 saw another flurry of activity, with Johnson clinching deals worth a total of $5.6 millions on Dodge Cleaners, formerly B & B of Nashville, with six high-volume outlets in the country music capital; Custom Cleaners Inc. of Savannah, Georgia, again with six shops; and Whitfields Inc. of Charleston, South Carolina, whose three large retail plants have been taken over by Coleman Young. Dodge was bought from Byron J. Begley, described by Philip Bollom as "a resourceful businessman with a background in a large family drugstore business in Lexington, Kentucky, and a very likeable and genial Southern gentleman." The deal also brought the group the services of his son Byron B., an alert and capable young executive who has stayed on as president and has also built up a chain of five retail printing outlets known as Insty Prints in the Nashville area. In January 1988 the Johnson Group made an interesting experiment in diversification when it acquired Insty Prints, too; the feeling is that there could well be scope to look further into this sector, for individual shops are service units managed very much along the lines of small dry cleaning plants.

Byron Begley Junior is in no doubt about the wisdom of the sale to Johnson. "It has made very little difference to the way we operate," he says. "Our accounting has changed somewhat, for the better, and we now have a reporting system in which we have to get certain facts and figures in to head office, and in due course they come back to us and give us the statistics for the whole group, and we can see how we've done compared with the other guys. So the changes have been positive, and capital is easier to get; we don't have to think about going to the bank any more, and all that that entails, we just talk to Jim Wahl about it. The Johnson Group acts as our bank. We're in the position now where we're the leading dry cleaners and leading instant printers in Nashville, but with the group behind us we're never likely to rest on our laurels, we'll always be looking to grow. Our plan in the next three years is to expand only in Nashville, but if something cropped up elsewhere and it looked right and the Johnson Group wanted me to get involved in it I'd go for it. Another advantage of group membership, one of the best, is getting to meet other members and exchanging information. If I'd had a problem before we'd been acquired by the Johnson Group I probably wouldn't have known how to handle it. Now I can call on up to twelve different people in the same situation I'm in and take their advice. I do that a lot. Of course folk do things in different ways, and what's right for one man is not always right for me. But after you've talked to two or three people and got their opinion it's not hard to pick the solution that would work best for you. And that's just one of many reasons why the Johnson Group has been a good thing for us."

After this flurry of activity the group acted fast again in July 1987 with a further move to strengthen its position in the Middle West, until that time its second strongest U.S. trading area after South Carolina and Georgia. It bought Pride Cleaners of Kansas City, with 41 outlets in Kansas and Missouri, for a total of $6.5 millions – and in so doing captured the services of its chairman Jim Barry, then just 40, who had built it into a business showing a profit of $753,000 on a $6.15 millions turnover in just a handful of years. Jim Wahl describes him as "one of the most organised men I've ever met, with tremendous leadership qualities", while Philip Bollom sees him as a major force in the industry. He became a U.S. Navy pilot after leaving college but returned to civvy street after only three years as the end of the Vietnam war left him and many of his peers surplus to requirements. His first venture was in Houston, Texas, where he quickly built up a janitorial supply business. Come 1982 he decided to buy out his partner or sell his interest, and as the partner was very keen to stay it was eventually Jim who moved on. His wife Barbara's father, Harry Hunzeker, had an interest in a dry cleaning franchise in Kansas City, and the more Jim Barry researched possible business opportunities, the more he became convinced that this was a line in which he could earn success by applying sound management skills.

He spent six months picking up the practical aspects and then he and Barbara were away on the great adventure that saw them opening or acquiring those 41 stores in little more than four years. Pride Cleaners was named by a leading American business magazine as one of the U.S.A.'s 500 fastest-growing companies, and with facts like that behind them it is no surprise.

Philip Bollom still has vivid memories of the talks leading up to the purchase: "David Seligman of the New York office of S. G. Warburg joined Jim Wahl and me in Kansas City. I recall the three of us in the large, comfortable kitchen of the Barrys' spacious home during the initial negotiations with Jim and his advisers, and being kept going by regular cups of coffee. Jim B. is a shrewd negotiator – and so is Jim W., for that matter – and it was some weeks before agreement was finally reached. In the event the Johnson Group acquired a splendid business and a top-class executive in Jim Barry." There was another step in the right direction a little later, in January 1988, when the big Duggins dry cleaning and laundry plant in Kansas City was bought for £842,697, and immediately integrated with Pride – and there was special significance in these deals in that they helped to push the Johnson presence in the U.S. above the 200 shops mark; the purchase came at the same time as the Insty Prints deal, which was worth £1.45 million. Not for the first time, the timing of these forays into the market was strongly influenced by the strength of the pound against the dollar.

The pattern of acquisition so far had been one of quite spectacular growth through a policy perhaps best summarised as "little and often". There had been the purchase of a number of chains of three or four dozen shops, but just as many of the group's excursions into the market had been for small family businesses with half a dozen outlets or fewer. The news of May 1988 put paid to that, when the Johnson Group clinched its position as the largest dry cleaner in Britain, the United States and the world by moving in for the Miami-based Dryclean USA for $30 millions-plus. It goes without saying that in this one stroke of business Philip Bollom and his board struck the biggest deal by far that the company had ever made, but with the pound still strong against the dollar the chairman saw the purchase as excellent value for money. Dryclean USA came with 79 company-operated stores in Florida and 153 franchise shops, mainly in Florida, Texas, California, Arizona and Wisconsin. "It is a growth-oriented quality company which we had identified as an acquisition target for some time," Philip Bollom recalls. "The business had been developed with skill and drive by the highly talented Eric Schwartz, to the extent that there were projected profits of $3.3 millions by 1988 and $5.4 millions by 1989. Jim Wahl paved the way when he carried out a financial appraisal of the business and held discussions with Eric and Damon May of the investment bankers First Equity Corporation, and by mid-April of 1988 Jim and I were able to fly to Miami to clinch the deal. On the evening before formal talks began we dined at the Grove Island Hotel with Eric, Damon and his colleagues Al Pereira and Bill Steiner, and on our side, Nigel Christie and John Gregg of Warburg's New York office. Damon had ordered his favourite Cuban dish for us all – grouper, a kind of sea bass, with rice and black beans. It was delicious, but the after-effects on me possibly served to give the other side some advantage!

"Friday started at 6.45 a.m. with a helicopter flight over Miami to give us a bird's eye view of the tremendous growth taking place in the area. This was followed by visits to a number of Dryclean USA stores, all very attractive and striking in their distinctive red, white and blue livery, immaculately clean and with add-on services promoted vigorously. I was left in no doubt that the average standard was as good as I had seen anywhere in the States, and most important of all was the obvious skill shown in site selection. They had gone for strip shopping centres in affluent areas, corner units if possible, and their shops were more similar in size and layout to their British counterparts than most in America. I confess, though, that what intrigued and attracted me most was the prospect of those 153 franchise stores, which were showing rapid growth and offering great potential. This deal bought us a strong and ready-made franchise team.

"We were ready to get down to preliminary discussions by late on the Friday afternoon. At the beginning we were a long way apart, but as the talking went on the gap narrowed, and by the next morning there was not too much between us. I flew back to Britain with the feeling that the remaining issues could be resolved, and that we would be in the position to resume serious negotiations within the next week. By the end of the month we were discussing the acquisition of the entire issued common stock of Dryclean USA for $29,750,000 plus a possible maximum $3.25 millions depending on certain profit targets being met, and after talking it over with Warburg's and our brokers Cazenove's, we concluded that the most suitable way of raising finance would be by issuing 11.5 million £1 convertible preference shares offered to existing shareholders on the basis of three for every five ordinary shares held. Those are the figures, but the quality of management is at least as important a consideration, and I immediately felt that in Eric Schwartz we had found another winner. He was 50 at the time of the acquisition, having been in the business since 1961, and I had no hesitation in recommending that he should be appointed a J.G.I. director. He is dynamic, as befits a man who built such a business from nothing in so short a time, but he is also genuine and straightforward, and I considered that his knowledge and ability would prove a great asset to the board."

The Dryclean USA purchase pushed the Johnson presence in America up from 200-plus to well over 400 almost overnight – and heaped yet more responsibility on the Johnson Group Incorporated board, which in early 1989 stood as Philip Bollom, chairman and chief executive; Jim Wahl, deputy chairman, president and chief operating officer; Michael Sutton, the U.K.-based group financial director; Bill Pulley; Coleman Young, replaced in the March by his son Cole; Mel Shapiro; Jim Barry; Eric Schwartz; and Gene Katterjohn. The latter is another valued contact from the Varsity Conference, the president of Owen Cleaners of Paducah, Kentucky, a company which he joined as a partner in 1951. A true Southern gentleman, courteous, cordial and dignified, he was born in Paducah in 1921 and served as an artillery officer and flight instructor of army aviation in the Second World War and Korea after graduating from Columbia Military Academy and Purdue University with a B.Sc. degree in pharmacy. Gene and his accomplished and cultured wife Carolyn are prominent in local civic affairs, and until recently he counted the chairmanship of the board of the Paducah Bank and Trust Company among his many responsibilities. "He brings a wealth of knowledge and commercial experience to the J.G.I. board," says Philip Bollom.

And then, of course, there is Jim Wahl, whom the chairman describes as "a man of great talent and drive, a tower of strength to me in the U.S.A., as well as a close personal friend, and a giant both in physique and character. His genial personality, co-ordinating skills and vitality have served us well in the development of our American operations, and I never cease to be struck by his extreme loyalty to and patience with an often impatient chairman!" Like so many successful people, in the Johnson Group and elsewhere, Jim enjoys the support of an understanding and encouraging spouse. Jerry Wahl is a charming and vivacious character of whom Philip Bollom says: "Her contribution far exceeds any limits of obligation or duty. She supplies a plus factor of genuine interest – and always with buoyant cheerfulness."

Now in his middle 50s, Jim Wahl gained a degree in business administration at Cincinnati University and worked for Procter & Gamble, W. R. Grace and Federated Department Stores before joining Apparelmaster Inc. in its infancy in 1972; Philip Bollom rewarded his efforts by nominating him a member of the full group board in 1987. A Johnson Group man through and through, he revels in his work and is tremendously excited by the prospects opened up by the Dryclean USA acquisition. "As chief operating officer I am in the position where all the companies report direct to me, but it really isn't that kind of relationship," he says. "It is more a case of my supporting them in their efforts to get more turnover and profit for the group, and I just want them to keep on doing the things they have been doing, so long as they remain successful. If nothing's going wrong, I'm not going to interfere, but if we've got a company that's not making the profitability I think it should make, then I will go in and get personally involved with it. I'm also the one who works with the head office staff in Cincinnati – a very streamlined and hard-working staff, I might add – and we can offer things for the companies which they might not be big enough to manage themselves. Right now in the United States, for example, hazardous wastes are becoming a big concern. An Act in 1988 decreed that every dry cleaning location in the country had to be identified, with the types of substances used in their plants fully specified. We did everything through central office, rather than let all our separate companies go off at tangents and waste time that would have been better spent on concentrating on cleaning and renting clothes, and that is just one recent and very specific way in which a group approach can save endless resources and effort.

"The group has a training function, whereby we instruct staff and they in turn go home and pass on what they've learned to their colleagues; we have an accounting function, and we will also support the various accountants at company level. Then, of course, we circulate the same sort of accounts for each of the companies, and I call it management by comparison. The heads of each company will look at the results every month and compare themselves with each other. If there's peer group pressure it's self-imposed, and that's the interesting part of it. There was one of the companies that didn't work out quite so well for us, and one of the first times I went in to visit it the man who sold it to us looked at me and got very defensive. He said gee, my rents would be lower if I were open 24 hours a day like those guys in Vegas, or I would be doing better if this happened or that happened, and that was purely because he saw himself in a bad light after seeing how he was doing against the other companies. I didn't have to say a word. I don't think we apply peer pressure from central office. There's one company I've had to spend a lot of time with lately because it isn't doing well, and the man in charge thinks I'm having a lot of pressure put on me. He said as much last time I was in there and I got a little mad about it. I said 'No, I'm not here for that reason, I'm here because I have the reputation of getting things done'. He said 'Well, I do, too'. It's interesting, ever since we had that talk he's been like a ball of fire, all charged up. That's the relationship I try to have. I try to work with them and be friends. I don't know whether that's supposed to be the best way, but it's worked for me. One thing I never forget is the fact that there are a lot of differences in the way you can run a dry cleaning company. We might have some people who feel that it would be more beneficial if we had a one-name operation all over the United States, but the autonomy we've given our companies, and the pride they have in having their own board, must count for something. I believe that if we were to change their names we might lose something. I'm happy to think of our operating in the same city with the Dryclean USA name competing with the Dodge name. If we're going to lose the business to someone else, I'd rather we lost it to ourselves. Perhaps if there's scope for any change at all, it will be in developing on a regional level – perhaps two or three separate regions in the Mid-West, one in South Carolina and Georgia, and one in Florida with Dryclean USA. I certainly wouldn't like to see that company split up in any way.

"I don't see any disadvantages at all in working in the U.S. for a British parent company. Philip Bollom and his predecessor John Crockatt are two completely different men, but I have enjoyed my working relationship with both. John Crockatt gave me all kinds of latitude, and was maybe not as detail-oriented as Philip Bollom, who likes to be very involved in everything and is very supportive of all of us in the U.S. The chairman's wife Sheila is also a very popular lady, and she sure softens P.B.'s image. With her warm personality she is unfailingly pleasant and cheerful, but it goes far beyond this. A very perceptive nature is another of her virtues, and sometimes her insights have proved invaluable.

"I have worked with big companies where we made acquisitions and six months later all the managers were gone. I didn't like that. Here we encourage management to stay, and it's worked out very well. There's a lot of *esprit de corps* and camaraderie; in the last year we instituted something called SCOPE, a special committee on priority expenditure which set out to get the best purchasing economies we could. We organised a sub board of directors, some of the younger fellows in the group, and when they met I felt there was sometimes something almost like static electricity in the room, the rap sessions we were having. It was really exciting and gratifying and I liked that. I think all these other fellows did, too. I'm sure a number of them will play a major part in group affairs in years to come."

There is little doubt that the success of sessions such as this stems to no small degree from the very special management style of Jim Wahl, who has done so much to help mould the character of the Johnson Group's growing empire in the United States. He is, as Philip Bollom says, a tower of strength; yet he is living proof of the fact that leaders who warrant such accolades can still be nice guys, too.

13 – Continuity, Growth and Profit

The Johnson Group's profit before tax in 1988 was £18.46 millions; thus, in five years, group profits were improved by 193 per cent, and turnover by 118 per cent. Return on sales rose from a low of 8.7 per cent in 1985 to 14.8 in 1988, and net assets over the same period grew by 92 per cent. This translated into a rise in earnings per share of 128 per cent since 1985; in '88 alone earnings rose by 54 per cent, from 39p to 60.1p.

This performance, together with the scale of the expansion into America, will go down as Philip Bollom's most spectacular achievement as chairman of the Johnson Group. But he looks back with satisfaction, too, at the progress made in the U.K. dry cleaning and textile rental market during his time at the helm, and at various administrative and social moves aimed at improving the lot of all workers, from senior management to the youngest school-leaver. He is quick to give credit to his board for their part in these achievements, which have been the result of consistent team work.

He set out his stall to the operating company managing directors on his appointment in July 1985. "It is central to Johnson Group Cleaners' operating philosophy and the way the group has developed that we have a decentralised management structure," he told them. "Each local board, under its own managing director, has a considerable degree of autonomy in the day-to-day running of its affairs, and it is my firm intention to retain this structure. In time it may be necessary to add strength to central support in some areas, but this will not signify any erosion of our present structure – indeed, the aim will be to enhance it.

"In group terms our objectives can be defined as continuity, growth and profit. The pursuit of growth implies profit, because that is required to finance expansion. The pursuit of profit implies growth, since the funds generated will be ploughed back into the business, and thus into its expansion. With profits and growth there won't be much doubt about continuity. The fact is that without growth we lose the dynamic of a company and the chance to give people opportunities. The business cannot afford to stand still, and so our prime requirement is the growth of an increasingly profitable business. If we are to be successful it must be the result of sound team work. I believe that together we can do a good job."

Accompanying his message was his statement of company principles, upon which he expanded at some length at the operating companies' annual general meetings of 1986. In brief, the statement set out to encapsulate the philosophy of the group in a simple framework within which every employee could work. "Some of it may have seemed a bit trite and self-evident, but it was all relevant and I am glad it was put in writing," he says today.

His first two principles applied to the group's relationship with its customers – "To provide quality, reliability and good value in the services we sell" and "To develop and maintain the right relationships between the company and its customers". Philip Bollom has long clung to the principle that service is all that a dry cleaner has to sell; there is nothing else. "There are scores of other dry cleaners around the country, each one trying one way or another to provide a service, so that is what we've got to sell, and sell it better than the rest. The service business is very rewarding if you make customer satisfaction your first priority, but by doing that you are not only making a fellow human being feel good – you are ensuring the survival of your company and your job, for they both depend entirely on the quality of what we have to offer. If we don't put the customer first, you can be sure that someone else will, and that applies to textile rental as much as to retail dry cleaning. When we make the Apparelmaster agreement with a customer we promise to provide a service better than anyone else in our industry. We make a number of specific service promises to him, and good service and good value mean keeping those promises. 'The customer is king' should be axiomatic in all our operations, and every function of the company should have as its prime objective the satisfaction of customer requirements. On the textile rental side the importance a company attaches to ensuring the customer is satisfied pays off in contract renewals. On the retail side we must be seen to be dealing with customers openly and fairly. There must be no indifference to customer problems, and this means swift and comprehensive attention to complaints."

The next two principles applied to profit: "To achieve high and increasing levels of profit, so enabling us to meet our responsibilities to shareholders and employees", and "To improve our competitiveness by constantly enhancing the performance of our production, distribution, selling, marketing and administrative functions". Philip Bollom believes that every company should show a high profit orientation, with all managers well informed about costs and profit and loss, and a high priority given to profit objectives. He feels the attention of the whole workforce should be focused on how employees' performance can affect the returns from their company, rather than simply their own immediate job. In quite a few cases workers really do identify with overall corporate goals, and he believes that more would become more closely involved through various measures – a higher degree of communication from management, incentives, a programme of promotion from within and a general air of respect for the individual in the working environment. On communication – "listening as well as talking, that's an absolute must" – he is a firm believer in the axiom that those who have no information can take no responsibility: "In addition to employee reports, weekly letters and so on, we should encourage communication by meetings and informal face-to-face encounters. Some of our companies are extremely good at this, and I believe it is no coincidence that they tend to turn in the best profit figures." Another means of improved communication, this time to shareholders, has been the introduction of an extensive colour review of the group's activities in the annual report. "I want the report to bring the group to life for shareholders, rather than simply list page after page of statistics," says Philip Bollom.

On incentives, he insists that schemes must be thought out carefully, and geared to profit. At grass roots level branch incentive bonuses obviously increase the interest the staff takes in the shop's weekly figures, while farther up the ladder, profit-related incentives bring a sharper edge to management attitudes. "As top managers, our approach to incentive payments must be objective," he says. "Assessment of management performance is based on the ability to produce satisfactory profits. Any other form of assessment is subjective." One of his first moves on becoming chairman was to draw up a package aimed at motivating the group's U.K. operating company managing directors and senior managers to maximise profit. The first element of this was a good basic salary. Next came a performance-related incentive scheme, with the minimum standard of performance required being a return of 10 per cent on turnover. To reach that target would qualify the manager for a bonus of 5 per cent of his annual salary – but he could earn anything up to 35 per cent extra for a really outstanding performance. Finally, the package undertook to set up an executive share option scheme, which would give senior management the opportunity to build up long-term capital accumulation in the company. "Together with planned organisational and personal objectives, it was just what we needed to spark the motivation we sought," Philip Bollom reports. "Within two years virtually every company was showing an improved performance – dramatically so, in certain instances."

On the question of promotion from within, the chairman sees three good reasons why it should be the first option: "As industry leaders, at least on the dry cleaning side, we should see ourselves as the harbour of best practice, anyway; it is easier to identify talent and potential from people within the organisation; and I view the concept as a means of keeping the people we want, and of extending the 'family' outlook. It is this that has made the Johnson Group what it is today, and it extends into my feelings about our need to show respect to the individual. I think it is true that we are perceived as caring employers. I certainly hope so, and that it continues to be so. Respect for the individual means, among other things, practising what we feel is right in terms of dealing with human problems. Part of the respect we have for people must find expression in making a reasonable response to a genuine need."

On the second profit principle, based on the improvement of competitiveness, Philip Bollom says that this essentially involves attention to detail: "When constant attention is paid to every aspect of the business we recognise our problems and mistakes, and so are in a position to take quick action to remedy them. That is the way to enhance our performance. Are production costs on textile rental right? If not, why not? What corrective action must be taken?

"Are collection and delivery costs right? If not, why not? What action should be taken?

"Are we achieving our sales objectives? If not, why not? Is it a selling problem? Is our marketing effective?

"That's the kind of thing. We need to be self-critical. That is the way to recognise our mistakes, and to make improvements."

People have always been central to the Johnson Group philosophy, and in his statement of principles Philip Bollom laid down two objectives: "To train and develop our people and to promote from within wherever possible; to recognise their individual achievements", and "To help them attain satisfaction and a sense of accomplishment

"Mel, I wanna clean every pair of pants in Las Vegas . . ." Phil and Mel Shapiro of Al Phillips the cleaners clown for the cameras in one of their many successful television campaigns.

Opposite: top – three Johnson Group chairmen and their wives: Jo and John Crockatt, Sheila and Philip Bollom and Nancy and Tom Johnson.

Bottom: a fun day in January 1986, when Mel Shapiro of the Las Vegas-based Al Phillips chain brought his wife Florence and mother-in-law Margaret Kelly to visit Bootle. Ms. Kelly is better known as the legendary "Miss Bluebell", whose early years were spent on Merseyside.

The Apparelmaster headquarters in Cincinnati, Ohio, and below Philip Bollom with the latest recruit to the J.G.I. board, Cole Young, who succeeded his father Coleman early in 1989.

Business Mail

Drycleaners group makes £18.5m

JOHNSON Group Cleaners, the company which owns the Zernys chain ...

has been strengthening its position in the United States over the past year. It bought up the Dryclean USA chain and franchise, giving it a total of 470 outlets in the US, and making it the largest coast-to-coast operation.

The total drycleaning turnover on both sides of the Atlantic was £89.5m, making for a trading profit of £13.3m.

its textile rental business.

Over the past year, Johnson's ...

Johnson cleans up with top earnings

MERSEYSIDE ... Group, which ... the world's bigg... ing group, ye... veiled record pr... Earnings soa... last year to £1 ... on the ...

Record profit for Johnson

JOHNSON GROUP Cleaners, the drycleaning company of which Pullars of Perth is an operating company, yesterday announced record pre-tax profits up by 59% for the year ... December 31, 1988.

earnings per sh... rose by 54% from 39p to 60...

Commenting ... group chair... Bollom said: record grow... pursue our growth an... both

Group turnover increased by 22.1% to £124 million and the ... improvement in operating ... continued.

Bollom helps Johnson to a record year

By Michael Bimpson

JOHNSON Group Cleaners ...

...y's figures ... turn-over up ... at £124.33 ... earnings per ... per cent to 23.1p ... 1987.

...7.9p final ... total to ... 1987.

Buoyant Johnson Group is poised to clean up in US

Robin Stoddart

JOHNSON Group Cl... transatlantic expans... paying off handsomely wider coverage boosts ability against a buoyan... nomic background.

The Merseyside-b... business, which leads the ... ket with 750 dry cleaning ... lets and is developing its ... chising acquisition in the U... lifting the dividend by a qua... after an earnings gain of m... than half.

cluding a final £1 million on ... sale of surplus ...

shares and business

Johnson success hits a new high!

Johnson Group's results ...

by 54% from 39p to 60.1p.

Commenting on the results, group chairman Phillip Bollom said: "1988 was a year of record growth. We continued to pursue our policy of organic growth and selective acquisitions both in the UK and the USA that fit within our existing structure."

... turnover increased 22.1% to ... the ... operating ... was continued.

... to pay a ... dividend ... firmed as ... per share ... for the ... compared ... 1987

Full marks chalked up for Johnson's Philip Bollom

CITY men do not have a reputation for lavish praise, but Mr Philip Bollom, who is at the helm of Johnson Group Cleaners, has won a worthy accolade for the half-yearly statement not only because of the profit record — up by 27 per cent excluding special items such as the net surplus of £112 000 on the sale of properties — but also because shareholders are given reasons for the group's success and future plans for expansion.

Johnson have 25 per cent of the UK drycleaning industry and rank as the largest in the US market.

Future acquisitions, Mr Bollom says, will be on a selective basis where they can strengthen existing operations on both sides of the Atlantic. He explains their success on efficiency and expertise, many of the group's senior executives, chemists and technicians, having been in the industry all their working lives.

Greater benefits are expected from takeovers already made in the US. In fact, Mr Bollom makes a particular point of emphasising his faith in America which offers "enormous scope for our future expansion."

Cleaning up . . . some of the many press reports spawned by the Johnson Group's trading success in recent years.

The clean, cool image of the 1980s: above, a Bollom shop in the South-west and below, the Southport branch of Johnsons designed by the high-flying American Hy Farber.

from their work; to seek to provide job security". Expanding on this, he says that if promotion is to come from within, then the onus of management development has to fall internally: "In a way, all managers are teachers, and it is important that they should set out to develop the people below them. Adequate attention needs to be given to the training function at all levels of the business, and to an extent I believe that we tend to be better at this on the textile rental side than on retail at present, perhaps because we are that much newer to it, and have all had to learn the ropes comparatively recently. As for helping people to attain job satisfaction, I am a strong believer in workers being given credit for a job well done to the same extent that they must expect to be ticked off for mistakes. It's so easy for employees to get in the way of thinking: 'The only time the boss takes any notice of me is when I do something wrong'. It's a well known fact that bad news sells newspapers. Ask a press baron why his paper concentrates on death and disaster, and he'll reply 'if we fill it with good news, nobody will buy it'. He's probably right. I seem to recall someone starting a good news paper a few years ago, and it failed miserably. But an unrelieved diet of bad news is no way to motivate staff. It is vital that they should believe that the company will give them credit where it is due and treat them fairly, for only then will they attain satisfaction and a sense of accomplishment in their work. They need to have confidence in our integrity and a positive attitude towards 'doing the right thing'. This leads to a feeling that we seek to provide job security."

There are three principles connected with management: "To provide objectives and leadership which generate enthusiasm"; "To practise management to the highest standards of competence"; and "To encourage initiative, enterprise and creativity. To emphasise what is to be done, while leaving room wherever possible for creative solutions compatible with the overall goal". As always, Philip Bollom has some forthright views on this issue. "Top management does not have to be liked to get the best out of people, but it helps," he says. "It certainly has to be respected and trusted, and in referring to a top management image I do not mean how people see the group chairman. The key is in who people see themselves working for. In the case of the Johnson Group, most people identify with the operating company they work for, and it is the local managing director and his fellow directors who take on the role of visible top management. The managing director and the directors closely associated with either the retail or rental operations need to spend more time out of their offices than in them. They do not know what is going on in their company unless they are out and about. For instance, the very knowledge that the managing director or some other director will be visiting helps to keep operational units on their toes. To be seen, to be interested and to be involved is the leadership that generates enthusiasm. Leadership must be for the benefit of the followers, not the enrichment of the leaders. The real leader has the ability to motivate his people to perform to meet his expectations.

"To set clear and reasonable objectives right the way down the line, and then to encourage and help people to achieve those objectives; that's the prime requirement, that's the way to build the confidence of employees in the top management team, and to gain their acceptance that the men and women above them know where they are taking the company, and why. Only when the managers down the line have clear objectives can they set about trying to make it happen. In the case of the Johnson Group the objective is to concentrate on dry cleaning and textile rental with the aim of distinguishing ourselves from our competitors by providing a superior standard of service. Then there is the principle of practising management to the highest standards of competence – at all levels. I believe a good manager must be able to handle people, have a positive attitude towards problem-solving, be knowledgeable, consistent and decisive. Prompt, though never rash, decision-making is the hallmark of a good manager. Obviously an important decision needs careful thought, and input from colleagues and specialists, but once the manager has assembled all the facts he must act with authority and confidence, without delay. Some of the brightest men I have known have failed to make the grade because of their inability to make firm decisions, not all of them on matters of any great importance. Everyday minor issues should be dealt with very quickly, many in a matter of minutes.

"A manager also needs to possess another attribute. He must be competent in implementing laid-down procedures. We see this vividly in the textile rental business, where strict adherence to our procedures spells the difference between modest results and good results. It also applies to the retail business, where adherence to systems and procedures is essential if we are to provide good service.

"I like to think the principle of encouraging initiative, enterprise and creativity will make managers think carefully about the thin dividing line between trusting people by delegating responsibility to the lowest level, so long as you are sure that the people there will use it effectively, and on the other hand, the abdication of management duty. Action and results must be monitored constantly. Such monitoring may well reveal mistakes and we must accept them, so long as we know that people have honestly tried. The true way to encourage initiative and enterprise is to give people responsibility and then to support them. The important thing is that top management is informed of what is being done, and why. This way it can be alerted to any possible problems. The big sin is not to let the top know when there is bad news.

"The last part of the final principle concerns setting goals while leaving the manager some scope to strive for them in his own way. In any company a manager's freedom to act is set against a background of restraints, some imposed from outside, like market conditions, and others set down by the company. We need to create an atmosphere in which these constraints can be turned on their head and be seen instead as opportunities, and one way in which top management can help do this is to ensure that petty and unnecessary restrictions are kept to a minimum. Our main concern must be focused not so much on how a particular manager does his or her job, but on performance against set targets. A manager needs freedom to manage in his own way, within a clear framework. There is no single blueprint for a successful manager and everyone, within limits, must do things his way. Performance is our concern, not the way in which results are achieved. We need to recognise the performance of the individual, to evaluate his or her strengths and to build on them. Obviously we must also consider what action is required in the case of the non-performer."

The final two principles laid down by Philip Bollom are concerned with what he terms the style of top management. "To be concerned with performance and results" and "To give operating companies reasonable freedom of action and to encourage them to make the fullest use of it. To attempt to combine the accountability, flexibility and freedom characteristic of a small company with the strengths of a large organisation". He explains that to achieve results there must be accountability, an individual manager must be accountable for his results. You cannot have such accountability without measurement, and it comes down to the fact that if an objective is delegated to a man he must feel a sense of obligation for its accomplishment. If it is accomplished he personally will enjoy the credit. If it is not, he knows he must face up to the opprobium. There must of course be monitoring systems, but Philip Bollom is certain that "accountability is meaningless unless it gets down to the personal feelings of the individual. A person must feel that it applies to him or her, and no-one else." On the freedom of operating companies within the group, the chairman restates his belief in the structure as it stands, rather than any move towards centralisation. "There are three good reasons for the separate company principle," he says. "The first is that in a relatively small business the people in charge know the employees, understand them and can be approached for explanations. Next, a small business has a manageable team of people who can be so intense in their interest that they can provide the best service, and the management can get the best effort out of the people who work for them. And finally, small businesses are sensible profit centres, and local boards are clearly responsible and accountable for the assets entrusted to them. Our business is all about local people and local management teams."

The strengths of a large organisation referred to in the last principle are the benefits of centralised finance, pensions, property dealings, information systems, health and safety, some training and, of course, purchasing clout. But the smaller company can score heavily in terms of flexibility, its speed of response to opportunities and its close involvement with its workers, and the correct balance of the two approaches – in other words, the creation and maintenance of the correct framework of central control and local autonomy – is vital for the group's long-term success.

Another feature of Philip Bollom's years in the chair has been a tight control of costs and overheads. The month after his appointment in the summer of 1985 he agreed with the board that there should be a simple strategy to stop operations that either lost money or failed to yield an acceptable return, devoting resources instead to projects that would prove profitable. "This meant, essentially, that we would concentrate on what we knew and did best, dry cleaning and textile rental," he recalls. "The most tangible effect was that we disposed of most of our laundries soon after this decision."

As Philip Bollom had always preached frugality during his eight years as group managing director, his announcement of a major blitz on cost control and overheads hardly came as a surprise to his colleagues on the board. "A pound saved is a pound more profit," he says. "It's a truism – but more than that, it's just plain true, isn't it? We're all in this business together. The more the company earns, the more we'll all stand to earn. That's the kind of creed we set about instilling in everyone involved in the business. We started with the senior people, and we agreed that the company aircraft should be sold. There had been a company aircraft for 20 years when I moved up, and in the early days it was said that it more than paid for itself. That's as maybe, but by 1986 our feeling was that it could not be fully justified on the grounds of cost, so in the end it had to go. Members of the board were asked to watch their personal expenses and reduce them, and so it went on down the line.

"Operating companies got the message loud and clear that the key to profit improvement was firm control on spending. Capital expenditure must result in a sound return for the company, and so projects have to be planned with the aim of squeezing the maximum return. Revenue costs are monitored closely, and stringent controls are placed on all expenditure and expenses areas. We made sure we were on the ball in reducing debtor balances, and in ensuring that cash settlement discounts were what they ought to be. I undertook to meet as many of our major suppliers as possible, working closely with our group purchasing officer, Don Atkins. As a result we were able to trim costs on numerous capital and revenue items; in fact, during 1986, we found ourselves paying no more, and in some cases less, than we did for the majority of items in 1985. That exercise certainly confirmed my earlier impression of Don as a man with potential, and in the following year I was pleased to be able to appoint him managing director of Apparelmaster Design."

From the above it will be clear that Philip Bollom brought a battery of forthright views on management principles and style to his years as Johnson Group chairman – but what impression of his own abilities will he leave on his senior colleagues, past and present? They are a diverse cross-section of men, their success in the dry cleaning business with the group being perhaps their main unifying factor, but time and again the same adjectives crop up when they discuss the outgoing chairman: "leads from the front"; "direct"; "decisive"; "to the point"; "energetic"; "enthusiastic"; "meticulous – incredible attention to detail"; "wants to be involved in everything – tremendously 'hands-on'". And flexible? "More flexible than some of those adjectives might suggest," a retired executive recalls. "He would walk into your office and say 'right, we're going to do this,

this and this', at which point you had three choices of action. You said yes or you said nothing, in which case you committed yourself to going along with it. Or you wasted no time in saying 'hey, I'm not sure that's a very good idea', and he would let you have your say, and if you put forward a strong enough case he would take notice. Decisiveness is the management quality he probably admires above all other. He himself has it in abundance – and if he recognises it in someone else, he will never be the one to disregard it or sweep it aside. If you've got right and sound sense on your side, and put your argument over with conviction, then Philip Bollom will always listen to you."

14 – *'They Look After You'*

"I think it is true that we are perceived as caring employers," Philip Bollom commented in the last chapter, and it has for generations been the company's aim to live up to that reputation. Times and social conditions change, and means of assuming at least some responsibility for employees' health and welfare must always be open to question and modification. There is no harm in being known as an old-fashioned firm if by old-fashioned the critic implies a degree of enlightened paternalism. But as with any other sphere of operations, there is no cause for satisfaction if your approach to staff relations begins to lag behind the times, and the Johnson Group has not let its pride in the past achievements of Sir Ben and others obscure the need for a constant review and updating of its welfare provisions.

Several companies within the group can point to acts of enlightenment from late Victorian times onwards, particularly those in which the Liberal or Nonconformist influence was strong. Up in Perth, Pullars built their first workers' houses in 1886 and added to them considerably in the ensuing years, strong little stone terraces with their roofscapes interspersed with forward-facing gables to add interest. In isolation these rows would have graced any squire's estate village in rural Britain, and though their effect *en bloc* was perhaps not quite so idyllic, they represented a standard of living hitherto unknown to most of their tenants. The houses put up in 1898 were named Klondike after the river valley at the heart of the great Canadian gold rush.

The year 1890 saw the formation of a swimming and life-saving club for workers and their families, and in 1895 Pullars set up a 40-piece Perth town band with instruments, stands, uniforms and music, as well as donating £200 a year for three years to help set it on its feet. Also in 1895 came a school for the children of workers which lasted until 1911, after which the building was converted to serve as the Tulloch Institute. And in 1897 the company's provision of a variety of rooms for rest and recreation led employees to show their thanks by presenting the directors with an illuminated address: "By a large expenditure you have furnished for our use Dining, Reading and Smoking Rooms. We now go on from week to week without the slightest cause of complaint, and with feelings of gratitude for benefits conferred." Both the perception of a smoking room as a social benefit and the Pullars workers' fulsome message of thanks smack of another age of staff relations, as does the company's decision in 1899 to grant a "few days'" annual holiday to men and women with service of 30 years or more – without pay, naturally. The arrangement became more formal in 1907, when plans were made for men with 30 years' service, and women with 24 years', to be given a full week off a year, but jubilation over this breakthrough was muted by a dispute with the company's women workers who had completed more than 33 years' service. They had been on the same wage of 75s. a month for 17 years, and the directors' first reaction on being asked for a rise was along the lines of "if it's been good enough since 1890, it's good enough today." The women's leaders detected a certain flaw in this argument, persevered, and eventually won the promise of an extra 5s. a week – seven years on, in 1914. It is against evidence of contemporary working practices such as this that any acts of enlightenment must be judged and appreciated. But before we leave Pullars, an incident from 1912 reminds us that a Liberal employer was not always a liberal one. An assistant timekeeper in Perth was dismissed for spending some office hours in unbecoming correspondence with a woman worker who had left to live in Canada. Conclusive evidence was produced in the form of the impression of writing on blotting paper (and presumably a mirror with which to read it), and although the full nature of the heinous message was never revealed, it was enough to earn him the sack.

Down in Bootle the Johnson brothers were also feeling their way forward in the field of welfare. For instance, the Shops Act of 1911, although not in fact applying to "the business of receiving goods for the purpose of being dyed or cleaned", was welcomed by the company in its provision of a half-day closing per week. Johnsons had been doing it for years in all but its Liverpool shops, which were brought in line with the rest with the passing of the Act. At very much the same time Ben Johnson and his brothers were becoming intrigued by the philosophies of some of the great Quaker industrialists, the Cadburys and Rowntrees and the rest, and in the Lever Brothers' Port Sunlight they had a revolutionary exercise in enlightenment on their doorstep. Sir Ben did not waste the opportunity to see what was happening there, and in 1907 he gave workers a glimpse of his philosophy in the first issue of the *JB Journal*, the company's pioneering house magazine: "We are united in a desire to make the firm of Johnson Brothers famous not only for its work, its scientific developments, its enterprises and its commercial success, but as an example in respect to its institution, its co-operative organisations and its just and liberal conception of what a really good business means to employers and employed alike."

These sentiments were more than morale-boosting words. As early as 1903 a men's sickness benefit society with a management committee of workers had been established, to be followed by one for women three years later; the country as a whole had to wait until 1912 for the National Insurance Act. In 1902 a works suggestion scheme was a first step towards greater shop floor participation, one built upon in so many ways in the years since then; on-the-spot dental treatment was introduced in 1906, along with a lunch service, and medical and chiropody care, ostensibly for workers who could not afford the services of a "panel" doctor, came two years later. Company pensions, the first non-contributory for shop floor workers and the second contributory for salaried staff, were introduced in 1904 and 1907; the latter year brought the formation of the JB Legion of Honour, for merit and long service; and by that time the working week had been reduced to 48 hours, comparing very favourably indeed with expectations in other industries. It is interesting that many of the most enlightened employers of Victorian and Edwardian days had a high proportion of female workers – the figure in the cleaning and dyeing industry traditionally hovers around 80 per cent – but whatever the moral and social pressures upon them to make life easier for "the weaker vessel", to cite just one of the implausible epithets applied to women at that time, it was not long before all workers benefited from their actions.

To help with some of the Johnson innovations a social secretary was appointed in 1906, and in spite of her status as a weaker vessel, she worked with energy and enthusiasm to pave the way for a host of further improvements. By the end of 1908 the Bootle works had its own four-acre recreation ground with separate pavilions for men and women and facilities for a variety of indoor and outdoor sports. There were societies for music, drama and poetry, while for some those hard-won holidays could be spent at the company's holiday home at Hoylake or at a summer camp for young men down among the pines and sand dunes at Formby. Both of these latter facilities survived for years after the last war, until the prospect of a week in Benidorm for 19 guineas suddenly cast the charms of the Costa Mersey in a less alluring light. A savings bank for workers was opened in 1906, and in 1912 a series of works bonus prizes that had been awarded for some years was supplemented by a profit-sharing scheme in the form of a wage bonus. The ultimate objective, however, was a concept very familiar in the late 1980s – the opportunity for workers to hold a stake in the company through shares. The arguments in their favour then were the ones that prevail today – the encouragement of a feeling of greater responsibility, a breaking down of "them and us" demarcations – and in 1914 the dream became reality with the issue of Johnson's first employees' participating preference shares. After 15 years well over £100,000's worth had been taken up, and at the peak of the scheme employee shareholders accounted for almost 15 per cent of the votes in the company. The shares were bought and sold at their nominal value of 5s., later 25p., but they carried the same dividends as ordinaries, and holders of 200 or more had full voting rights.

It was a bonus that served the company and the workers well for threescore years and ten – until the time of the Nottingham Manufacturing takeover bid in 1984, in fact, when this survivor of pre-First World War industrial paternalism came face to face with the brash new world of corporate wheeling and dealing. Although it was never designed as such, the scheme handed down by Sir Ben and his brothers could be seen as an effective device for obstructing unwelcome takeover bids, and several City institutions were not slow to tell the group as much. "We feel that the employees' share scheme is an anachronism, and whatever its original intentions, it is now perceived mainly as a means by which the company can make things difficult for a potential predator," one fund manager concluded. "We are not saying that we would like to see the Johnson Group taken over, and indeed we were not tempted by Nottingham's recent offer, but we do find it hard to accept your justification for the scheme..."

Senior Johnson executives lost no time in meeting with Warburg's to discuss tactics, and it was agreed that unless changes were made the group could no longer count on institutional support when it came to fighting off any future takeover bids. Two courses of action emerged from the talks: to examine the share option schemes available, and to seek to convert the employees' shares into ordinary shares. It was obvious that this, in effect, would add up to a substantial capital gift to employees, and if it was done on a one-for-one basis there were fears from the start that some of the major institutions might not like it. Whatever change was finally agreed would call for a 75 per cent class vote in favour by the 1,200 employee shareholders, who by that time held some 2.2 million shares.

The matter was high on the agenda when Philip Bollom became chairman in the summer of 1985, and by October tentative proposals had been prepared. The plan was indeed for a one-to-one conversion of employee shares to ordinaries, together with a modern savings-related and tax-effective share option scheme to replace the old system on an ongoing basis – but all too soon fears that the City would not like it proved well founded. The proposals were said to make a "gift" of around £4 to the holder of each employee share, and the first big institution asked for its opinion saw this as unacceptably generous. It said that if the group proceeded with one-for-one it would vote against, and use all its influence to persuade its fellow corporate shareholders to do the same. Further research soon proved that other City institutions would indeed have needed no persuading to oppose the plan, so it was back to Warburg's and the drawing board. Four men sat around the table, Philip Bollom, the recently appointed financial director Michael Sutton, Arthur Winspear and his successor as Warburg's Johnson expert, Stephen Latner, and it was agreed that Messrs. Bollom and Latner should visit a number of major shareholders to argue the group's case and explore possible avenues of compromise. So began a series of meetings that took up a good part of 1986. Most contacts were helpful, notably Hugh Jones of Prudential Portfolio Managers; but the fund manager of the first institution approached for an opinion remained implacably opposed to any idea of conversion, and adamant that employee shares did not carry any capital entitlement over and above the basic 25p. Since the Panel on Takeovers and Mergers had ruled that in bid situations employee shares were equity capital, and should thus receive an offer providing a comparable capital sum, the messages from the experts could not have been more confused, but by early 1987 a widely acceptable solution was reached. It involved conversion on a one-to-one basis to avoid a reduction in capital, but would be combined with a capitalisation issue to holders of ordinary shares at the ratio of three new shares for every seven held. A savings-related share option scheme and an executive option scheme conforming with Inland

Revenue and IPC requirements would also be introduced, and when the proposals were put to an extraordinary general meeting in May 1987 they were carried by a large majority. The group certainly believed that, taking all into account, the terms were fair and reasonable. For ordinary shareholders there would be benefit from the effect of the conversion and capitalisation issue on earnings per share; from the incentive effect of the new option schemes; and, to play devil's advocate, from the removal of a potential barrier to a future takeover. As for the ex-employee shareholders, they would suffer a dilution of their voting rights, an initial income reduction and possibly a charge to taxation, but would be compensated by being able to realise the capital value of their holding through the market, and by the introduction of the new option schemes.

At much the same time, in September 1987 an actuary's three-yearly valuation showed both the group pension schemes to be in a healthy condition. As a result a package of benefit improvements was implemented, and a new contracted out money purchase scheme was introduced; for the first time this included part-time employees. A company contribution holiday was declared for both schemes from April 6, 1987, and from the same date all staff scheme members in service were granted a spouse's pension to cover all past service. Previously only widow's pensions were provided, and then only for service since April 1978. Pensionable salary was newly defined as the last twelve months' basic pay, instead of being averaged over the last three years, and staff scheme pensioners benefited, too. In addition to a 4½ per cent increase granted in 1988, all who retired before April 1980 had special increases to bring their original pension into line with inflation since they first retired. As the group had already introduced additional voluntary contribution schemes as far back as 1979 and 1985, it was well prepared for the new provisions of the 1986 Social Security Act, which made membership of all company pension schemes voluntary. "We owe much to Miss Angela Smith, a director of Johnson Group Management Services, for her expert administration of these pension schemes," says Philip Bollom. "It is an exacting responsibility, which she discharges with skill and no small degree of dedication."

The next step forward came early in 1988, with the introduction of a group occupational health scheme. "I had been considering something along these lines for some time, and had discussed it at length with Dr. David Thomas, then our industrial physician,"

Philip Bollom recalls. "I took my proposals to the board in the February and it took effect from March 1, with Dr. Thomas becoming group medical officer for a brief period."

The group believes an occupational health service should aim to attend to every aspect of safety, health and welfare for workers at all levels; to generate a sense of health awareness, which will in turn lead to an increased feeling of wellbeing and higher morale, to the benefit of the company; to set a reasonable health standard for people entering the company; to keep a watch on chronic health problems and long-term sickness absence; to monitor the use of toxic substances and potentially dangerous machinery, and analyse accidents at work; and to keep abreast of developments through liaison with academic centres which specialise in industrial medicine.

Education on preventative medicine is seen as a particular responsibility; without trying to kindle fear or intrude unduly on people's rights to privacy over their attitude to health, women employees are urged to take advantage of screening for breast and cervical cancer. During a pilot scheme conducted in Bootle in recent years the group has already helped identify more than an average number of suspect cases. Regular examinations for senior executives are another routine feature of the doctor's work; they tend to take the form of insurance company medicals, with additional tests of the respiratory function and full blood and urine screening, and frequent dental and optical checks are also encouraged.

The group has adopted an aim of seeking to improve the general health and wellbeing of all its employees. One of the ways of measuring its success over the longer term is by comparing the incidence of short-term sickness and long-term illness of its employees against the national averages. The objective is to reduce the group's figure to one well below the average by a combination of health education, preventative health screening and counselling employees on their health and medical concerns. Such a feat is difficult to achieve in service industries because of relatively high staff turnover, but the group's attitude, reflecting a company tradition of welfare stretching back a century or more, is that it is a worthy goal for which to strive.

15 – *The Essential Challenge*

Ivor Bollom left many lifelong legacies with his children, and his religious beliefs were chief among them. As we have seen, his elder son David eventually turned his back on commerce to devote himself to the Anglican Church, but Philip has upheld his father's approach, throwing himself equally wholeheartedly into business and the life of an active Nonconformist layman.

"Sunday, for me, is a day set aside from the rest of the week," he says. "It is a day for religion – not, of course, the only day for religious contemplation, but a special day, for all that. Religion sets a man at life's central task of dealing with himself, and it seems to me that this is its essential challenge. The most important truth about a man is that he has been entrusted with himself. This is a personal responsibility that cannot be dodged. I cannot claim anything but very limited success in responding to the challenge; but in spite of many failures, I know I must hold on to Christianity.

"I am fortunate in having come under the influence of some fine ministers. R. W. Waddelow, Penry Davies and William Cobley at Broadmead Baptist Church in Bristol were all men of stature to whom I have cause to be grateful. And in later years I owe much to Derek Thomas at Southport for many penetrating and thought-provoking sermon themes.

"During my life I have met a number of people who have little time for the church because they say they find too much hypocrisy among Christian people. Hypocrisy is a failing that is by no means restricted to those with religious beliefs. Hypocrites flourish in all areas of society, and people bring to religion the same human weaknesses they bring to all their relationships; because the church is composed of human beings, it must follow that there will indeed be some hypocrisy in its makeup. But no sensible man judges any area of reality – business, industry, education, politics or religion – on the basis of its weakest representatives, or in terms of what other people have made of it. He looks at the reality itself, its history, its accomplishments, its place in human life, and it is on these criteria that he must form his appraisal.

"For me, religion is reality. My conviction is that without God, life has no rational meaning. God alone guarantees that the world is not an orphanage, life is not a sad mistake, and death is not a dead end. Years ago I read the story of a frail little man from Japan called Kagawa. He was born in the slums, the child of a temporary infatuation between a dancing girl and a typical example of the military caste of the nation, both of them Buddhists. As it soon became clear that his mother would have nothing to do with him he fell into the clutches of his father's legal wife, whose resentment of his presence showed itself in constant humiliation and bullying. For twelve years Kagawa was her household slave, and by all known rules he should have grown up into a life of brutality and loose living. Somewhere along the way, however, he met Jesus Christ, and a miracle took place. He became a devout Christian, accepted responsibility for himself and made of his life something that commanded respect. I look to men like him – indeed, on occasions, I have been privileged to have met men like him – and I am convinced that Christianity has an argument to which this age can listen. Churches that speak out with vigorous authority on matters of faith demand attention, and today these are the churches with full and active congregations."

There were times in the difficult 1960s when the affairs of Broadmead Baptist Church made heavy demands on Philip Bollom, who was its general secretary from 1959 to 1967, chairman of the trustees from 1967 to 1981 and chairman of the Broadmead Building Trust from 1954 until 1988. He was also a trustee of Bristol Baptist College, from 1959 to 1983, and was for many years the chairman of its financial committee.

As he entered his thirties he found himself increasingly involved as a member of the congregation, a committed and questioning Christian who at the same time was comfortably at home in the business life of the city. He was a Round Table member, later a Rotarian, but most of all he was a keen and astute businessman who knew his way around the financial statements and the negotiating table, and at that time those were the kind of skills the Baptists of Broadmead needed.

It was an old church, with traditions as a chapel stretching back centuries into Bristol's colourful past, but the early post-war years saw it in a tremendous state of flux. It stood in the heart of the old city area devastated by the blitzes, a place of narrow streets once teeming with both business and domestic life; but the city planners' answer to this scene of desolation was to sweep away all but the most historic remaining buildings and the lines of the main thoroughfares and introduce a shopping centre that owed nothing to the past. Today the name Broadmead is synonymous with the "High Street U.K." section of Bristol's strangely fragmented shopping facilities, the spot for all the big department stores and household name chains.

Thus it was that in the 1950s and '60s the church, by that time showing serious and potentially dangerous signs of age, was on an extremely valuable building plot. So were neighbouring shop premises owned by the Broadmead Baptist Building Trust, and with developers sniffing around and showing ever keener interest, it was vital for the chapel that they should be met on equal terms. It could well have been that the property companies' negotiators went along to see the Baptists expecting to steamroller their way gently through a small committee of unworldly people. But whatever they were expecting, what they got was Philip Bollom.

Negotiations for the sale of the church's property were complex, tangled and hindered mightily by external influences. The first approach by a developer came in September 1961 from a company called Land Improvements Ltd. There were many differences between the two parties, while over at the Council House, as Bristol calls its town hall, it often seemed that planning applications had been sunk without trace. Eventually agreement was reached in April 1965, but hopes of an early start to a development with shops on the ground floor and a new church above were dashed within weeks.

"The Chancellor of the Exchequer announced the introduction of a building licensing system which applied to all privately-sponsored building projects costing more than £100,000," Philip Bollom recalls. "It was not until the end of November that the method of application for licenses became known, but we got in immediately and won authorisation for the project so long as work started before the end of 1966. It was fine with us, since we had a revised date of August '66 in mind – but that was a terrible trading year, with the freeze and a bleak economic outlook, and in the July Land Improvements became so nervous about the future that they pulled out. It was not a very happy way to end nearly five years of negotiation.

"We acted quickly, approaching a number of property firms and finally opening negotiations with the Laing Development Co. They were prepared to contribute £150,000 plus fees so long as the site was

The Bollom factory at Novers Hill, Bristol in 1968.

The shirt service at Bollom's modern plant in Southmead Road in 1988.

The Johnson Group board as at early 1989. Standing: Richard Zerny, Jim Wahl, John Mason, Michael Sutton. Seated: James Fox, Terry Greer, Philip Bollom, David Fowler and Arthur Winspear.

Terry Greer, who succeeds Philip Bollom as Johnson Group chairman in September 1989.

The Johnson Group Inc. board and senior executives as at early 1989. Standing: Donna Moore (senior executive), Mel Shapiro, Michael Sutton, Eric Schwartz, Jim Barry, Gene Katterjohn, Coleman Young, Mark Nocito (senior executive). Seated, Jim Wahl, Philip Bollom and Bill Pulley. Coleman Young has since been replaced by his son Cole, and below; Jim Wahl, Philip Bollom and many of the principals of operating companies in the United States.

Philip Bollom makes a retirement presentation to Sid Tuchman, a J.G.I. board member from 1982 to 1987 and a key figure in the group's early success in the U.S.

Off we go again . . .Mrs. Sheila Bollom has shared many of her husband's travels both at home and in the United States during his years as chairman.

leased to them for 125 years at a reasonable ground rent subject to periodic reviews. Again, shops were to be provided at street level, with the church on the upper floors. As the total cost of the building was estimated at £190,500, the church trustees were faced with the prospect of finding £40,000-plus, as well as a proportion of the fees, and with this in mind we made the decision to sell the shops owned by us, along with the church entrance in Broadmead. Laing's paid a total of £107,000 for these, £82,000 to the building trust for the shops and £25,000 to the church trustees for the entrance. Not that we saw much of the £25,000, since we paid it back to Laing's as a contribution towards the cost of the redevelopment. The building trust added £17,800 to this, but even after meeting certain expenses and making a £20,000 donation to the church for new fittings and furnishings we still came out of the deal with a healthy balance for investment. In fact the eventual building costs amounted to £225,000, but Broadmead's contribution remained at £40,000. The church today is insured for £1 million.

"This all sounds like the end of the story. It was not. The consent of the Charity Commissioners was needed, and it did not come automatically because of problems associated with five small charities administered by the church trustees, one of them dating from 1720! There were also one or two legal snags, but rebuilding finally began in 1967. In the February of that year we found temporary accommodation in Arley Chapel, an Italianate little Victorian building slightly north of the city centre, but it was sold to Polish Roman Catholics within twelve months, and we moved on to a disused chapel in Hotwells, to the west. Eventually, after nearly three years in exile, church members were delighted to be able to come home to the new Broadmead on October 4, 1969."

Two years before this date, in the autumn of 1967, Philip Bollom stepped down from his post as general secretary, though he remained as chairman of both the chapel and the building trust. By this time building work was well under way and the road ahead was clear for the church, while outside in the business world he needed all his resources to face up to the rigours of Selective Employment Tax and other external pitfalls as managing director of Bollom. In a presentation made to him by the Rev. Penry Davies and the congregation, however, he was left in no doubt that his labours on their behalf had not gone unappreciated. "His fellow members will ever recall his unfailing and meticulous care of details both large and small," their address read. "His public reports were a source of frequent inspiration, and his secretarial duties were discharged under the influence of a clear Christian commitment. In the long centuries of the history of Broadmead, he was seen to be God's man for the hour."

It was not until he became Johnson Group chairman in 1985 that he moved his home from Bristol to Merseyside, but he had been managing director for eight years before that, and the demands of that post and the travelling involved had taken their toll on his domestic life in a variety of ways. The most saddening was his separation from his first wife Patricia in 1977, to be followed by divorce a few years later. "Pat is a good woman who did a fine job bringing up our family," he says. "We have four wonderful children: Ian, director of finance at the National Trust, who is married with a boy and a girl; Anne, who lives in Monte Carlo with her husband Richard, a marine engineer, and also has a boy and girl; Pat, who is still in Bristol, married to John, a civil servant and busy looking after three children; and Peter, who is not yet married. We were particularly proud when all four of them got to university, and that was a feeling we could share. Unfortunately, though perhaps understandably, Patricia could never find herself as deeply interested in my business career as I was, and I am afraid that in time we just drifted apart. I know now that I was the difficult one."

Philip Bollom remarried in 1984, at Broadmead Baptist Church. "My wife Sheila has a wonderfully calm temperament," he says. "She is a great support, and an outstanding hostess. She has built up a considerable knowledge of the business and my various activities, and constantly proves herself my most severe and constructive critic. I owe her more than I can put into words."

He also pays tribute to a succession of excellent secretaries over the years, notably Mrs. Eileen Cammidge in Bristol, and more recently Mrs. Sheila Sill on Merseyside. "Both are extremely efficient, meticulous in their attention to detail and notable for their willingness to put up with me," he explains. "I have been able to function better because of their abilities, and I am grateful to both of them."

He finds himself very much at home with the Johnson Group philosophy. It parallels much of what he learned in his early years in the family firm from his father Ivor, and it fits in with many of his lifelong beliefs. "The group has always tried to treat staff, suppliers and customers honestly and fairly," he says. "It strives at all times to give the high standards of service the customer has a right to expect. Our success in meeting those expectations depends on the calibre of our staff and the way in which they discharge their duties. They cannot be expected to work hard and give the company their loyalty without good human relations at work. People are our priority – their development, their interest and their welfare. During my years as chairman scarcely an evening has gone by, when I have been at home, when I have not sat in my study for an hour to plan the next day. In the morning I have been ready to go and to set the pace, for the pace set by the man at the top is the pace of his team.

"Positive thinking is obviously the keynote – but it is backed up by a list of ten personal 'don'ts' that have stood me in good stead over the years. The first is don't accept outside directorships, and limit other outside involvements – most of my energy is necessary to run my own company; next comes a very similar one, don't get too involved personally with trade associations, but delegate that responsibility as far as possible; don't mislead anybody; don't mislead yourself; don't hide mistakes; don't neglect to study and follow professional management principles; don't complicate issues – aim to simplify them; don't waste time on small details someone else can attend to; don't make a decision before knowing all the facts – then decide, and stick to it; and finally, don't waste time, but manage it. As Ten Commandments go, they may seem a little negative; but they have worked for me."

16 – Valued Colleagues

Philip Bollom's years in the chair of the Johnson Group have seen the retirement of a number of friends and colleagues alongside whom he worked happily for many years – but he steps down in the knowledge that the senior management team he leaves behind is as strong as any in the history of the company.

His first task as chairman in the summer of 1985, before any thought could be given to such wider issues as expansion in America or the build-up of the U.K. textile rental market, was to consider a replacement for Norman Crockatt, forced by ill health to retire from his post as group technical director while still in his late 50s. A cousin of the former chairman John Crockatt, and his deputy Mr. Allan, who himself had stepped down for health reasons in 1983, Norman Crockatt had served the group well since he became a trainee at Eastman in 1949. He came with a degree in engineering after studying at Charterhouse and Imperial College, London, and to that was added a thorough and practical grounding at Eastman, followed swiftly in 1952 by Crockatt, Pullars and Flinn. In November 1952 came his first significant move, when he became technical manager of Lush and Cook, and it was not long before he rose to the post of general manager, as well as becoming a director of Flinn; it was in 1967 that he transferred to Bootle as chairman of the group technical committee, as well as gaining a place on the Johnson Brothers board. Some years later he joined the board of Johnson Group Management Services as group technical director, at the same time upholding a record of distinguished service in the wider dry cleaning industry. In 1978-'79 he served as Prime Warden of the Dyers' Company, and he was chairman of the Dry Cleaners' Research Organisation at the time of its merger with the launderers' equivalent, the B.L.R.A. The success of that merger owed much to his hard work and tact, which was apt since it was his father Arthur Crockatt who had inspired the formation of the D.C.R.O. Now living in retirement with his wife Stella, Norman Crockatt leaves Philip Bollom with memories of him stretching back more than thirty years. "What I recall most about him was his wonderful feeling for people," says the chairman.

"He had a reputation well beyond the group for being helpful, courteous and a friend, more than a mere colleague, and added to this was a depth of knowledge and application that made my regard for him and my admiration of his work grow increasingly over the years. It was a source of real sadness and concern when I discovered that my first task on arriving at Bootle was to get to grips with the fact that we would have to get by without his know-how, skill and wisdom."

Norman Crockatt's successor as group technical director, with a seat on the Management Services Company board, was Keith Ineson, a Johnson Brothers man since 1956. For the 15 years before his promotion he had been J.B.'s technical manager, but his other roles since his early days as a chemist in the dyehouse and dry cleaning departments had included those of health and safety and training officer. The group appointment was very much a logical progression of his work in fibre and fabrics, and one that had been very diligently earned. "He is doing an outstanding job for us," says Philip Bollom.

That summer of 1985 brought another shock when Sands Johnson, by then a group director and managing director of the Johnson Group Cleaners Property Company, suffered a heart attack in the July. He was not yet 50 and the early hope was that he would recover and return to his duties, but towards the end of the year it was decided that early retirement would be the most sensible course of action. The phrase "the end of an era" is a hackneyed one, but in this case it had more than a ring of truth, for Mr. Sands' departure left the company without a Johnson actively involved in the business for the first time in 169 years. The happy ending is that he and his wife Daphne are indeed enjoying an active and happy retirement, pursuing their interest in golf, travel and a variety of other activities; and not surprisingly, he and his father Mr. Tom continue to take the closest interest in the firm that bears their name. Mr. Sands is something of an authority on Johnson Brothers and group history, with boxes and cases of documents and photographs in his study.

After school at Malsis Hall and Uppingham, he joined the family firm as a trainee at Bootle in 1956, following two years of National Service that saw him commissioned as a second lieutenant in the Royal Artillery. "I heard quite a lot about Sands before I actually met him," Philip Bollom recalls. "When Bollom's joined the group way back in '55, Mr. Tom became company chairman and visited us for a couple of days every month. Sands was still doing his National Service in the early days, but his name cropped up frequently in conversation. It seems he was quite an athlete in those days, a long-distance runner who represented the B.A.O.R. in the army sports." In 1958 he attended the American National Institute of Dry Cleaning at Silver Springs, Maryland, and after two years of general work in the factory, offices and branches he was appointed manager of Johnson Brothers' service department; various other managerial appointments followed before he became a J.B. director in 1964. From 1965 to 1968 came a spell at Crockatt in Leeds punctuated by a management course at Henley, and when he returned to Bootle it was with responsibility for unit shop development with Johnson Brothers, working closely with the branches director, David Fowler. He became a director of the Property Company and a member of the property management committee in 1971, and took over as managing director of the property company in 1975 after two years as deputy. "For ten years he was responsible for the considerable property interests which form such a substantial part of the group's assets," says Philip Bollom. "It was a responsibility he discharged with skill and dedication. He also became a trustee of the Johnson Charitable Trust and the Employee Benefit Trust and in January 1981 he was appointed to the group board. We could always rely on him for a thoughtful, shrewd deliberation, and his seemingly endless work at the time of the hostile bids will always be remembered with gratitude. That astute judgement of his combined with a blend of common sense, independence of outlook and dependability to make him a good friend as well as an able and loyal associate. It was not just for historical reasons that the group's final break with the Johnson family came as a blow and a sad loss."

Sands Johnson played a major part in trade association activities, culminating in his presidency of the Association of British Launderers and Cleaners in 1980–'81, and his chairmanship of the A.B.L.C.'s dry cleaning and public relations sections. He also sat on the Industrial Relations Committee and the Laundry Wages Council, and his long-standing concern for the environmental problems associated with the dry cleaning industry found voice – in the English, French and German languages – in his involvement with the *Comité International de la Teinture et du Nettoyage*, of which he was technical committee chairman for a decade, vice-president and finally, in 1985, president. Away from work he is a Justice of the Peace, like his father Mr. Tom and his great-uncle Sir Ben before him, and among several charitable duties was his chairmanship, for several years, of the Brunswick Boys' Club. As for his leisure pursuits, one has only to look around his study at an intriguing range of golfing memorabilia to know that the links at Formby still play a vital part in his life.

Sands Johnson was replaced as managing director of the property company, and shortly afterwards as a main board member, by John Mason, a chartered surveyor who first came to the chairman's notice when he joined the Bollom company in Bristol in 1976. He became a Bollom director three years later and found a seat on the board of the Property Company in 1982, so he was well equipped to take responsibility for the group's large real estate portfolio when his time came in 1985. "He has performed very well," says Philip Bollom. "He is forceful and able, intelligent and energetic, and he has never allowed his involvement at the sharp end of the company's affairs to obscure a strong social conscience. Some far-reaching changes were introduced under him, with the management of the property departments transferred from the various operating companies to the property company. The intention was that the centralised company should provide a complete property service on a geographic rather than individual company basis, and after further refinements the change has resulted in a more cost-effective, efficient and professional approach that has been welcomed throughout the group." Outside office hours John Mason is a family man who enjoys a variety of sports, golf, swimming and squash among them.

The next boardroom move was not long to follow, for in September 1985 Michael Sutton, who came to Bootle in 1979 as group management accountant, rose from his post of company secretary and chief accountant to become the Johnson Group's first full-time finance director. "I look back on his promotion as an inspired appointment," says Philip Bollom. "He is a first-class financial director who carries out his duties with energy, flair and considerable success. He has the happy ability of being able to propose solutions rather than simply pose problems, a skill for which accountants are not universally noted; and all his colleagues share an admiration for his quick and alert brain and financial acumen. His administrative competence combines with an appetite for hard work to ensure that he never fails to deliver his figures, statistics and reports on time. And as if this were not enough, his moving up paved the way for another very bright and able young accountant, Yvonne Monaghan, to make her mark as company secretary and group management accountant. Mike Barnsley, a director of Johnson Group Management Services, manages the computer department and is responsible to Mike Sutton. His skill and expertise, allied to assiduous attention to detail, have made a major contribution to the success of our information systems."

Following almost instantly on this move, in October 1985, was the decision to promote Alan Linegar to the position of joint managing director of Bollom, the group's largest operating company, which covers large tracts of the South of England and Wales and had grown rapidly in various directions since James Fox had taken on the role of sole managing director in 1977. To add to his responsibilities, Mr. Fox had been a member of the main group board since 1983, and it seemed logical to share such a widespread geographical area between Bristol and the company's eastern base in the old Flinn H.Q. at Brighton. At Bristol Alan Linegar, who arrived from Sketchley as general manager in 1981 after 20 years in the industry, has responsibility for shops in Wales and the South-west, while James Fox's eastern area stretches from Bournemouth to London and the Kent coast. As with other managing directors, they find textile rental an increasingly significant responsibility, and by chance, both have seen major changes at their regional H.Q.s. In the West Bollom have moved their offices from central Bristol to the suburban premises of the former Clifton Cleaning, a substantial workwear rental operation acquired by the company in October 1986 and now completely modernised. And in Brighton, an extensive redevelopment of the Fishergate factory should see the £1.5 million bill almost covered by the sale of four small new warehouse units on the site in 1989.

"James Fox has come a long way since he started with Johnson Brothers as a management trainee in 1956," says Philip Bollom. "He has wide experience in all aspects of the business, and he is a valued colleague. I find him intelligent and jaunty, with an astute eye for furthering the company's interests. Both he and Alan are very energetic and highly motivated executives, and the closer attention they were able to give to their respective regions very quickly made its mark on the trading account."

Another chapter in Johnson history came to an end in August 1986, when Bill Davidson left after 48 years' service. He had a unique claim to fame, being the last person interviewed for a job by Sir Ben Johnson, very shortly before the grand old man's death in 1937; but if the truth be out, Bill Davidson had a wealth of claims to fame throughout the industry, and to many people outside the group he was thought of as simply "Mr. Johnson". He followed his district superintendent father into the company in 1938, but was called up the following year and spent the Second World War in the Royal Tank Regiment, rising to the rank of major and winning the M.B.E. for carrying out his duties, "often under fire and very difficult conditions, in a spirit of cheerfulness and selflessness which was an inspiration to everyone around him". The pattern remained the same for the rest of his working life.

He returned to Bootle for training in 1946, and in the following year he embarked on spells as district superintendent in Liverpool and York before returning to Merseyside in 1953 as head of the inquiry department. "In 1955 he was appointed assistant to the works director, and it was then that I first met him," Philip Bollom recalls. "It was at the time my family firm entered the group, and I remember his being referred to as one of Johnson's promising young men. I recall him as a slim young chap with a mop of black hair, always running around. The hair didn't quite last the course, but I remember him running to the end of his working days." Bill Davidson devoted the prime years of his working life to the Harris company in Birmingham, taking up his duties as works director in 1958 and serving as managing director from 1966 to 1974. Then followed two years as managing director of the towel hire division, and in 1977 came his elevation to the group board. In his later years he served as group safety officer and chairman of the group health and safety committee, and to the end of his career he upheld an influential role in the wider dry cleaning industry. He served as a council member of the Dyers and Cleaners' Research Association from 1960 to 1977, with three years as chairman from 1970 to 1973, and also saw sterling service with the British Launderers' Research Association, the Northern and Midland Counties Association of Dyers and Cleaners and the national council of the A.B.L.C., of which he was president in 1975–'76 and a long-serving health and safety committee chairman. Health and safety was also his speciality during his years on the council of the British Retailers' Association, and as chairman of the working party on dry cleaning guidelines he made a considerable impact on the Health and Safety Executive's view of the industry. After retirement Bill Davidson remained active as chairman of Sefton Council for Voluntary Service, as a fund-raiser for the Southport Hospice, an enthusiasm shared by Sands Johnson, and as the first independent chairman of the Fabric Care Research Association, and he left the company with high hopes of playing a little golf, walking his dogs and helping his wife of more than 40 years, Jeanne, in the garden of their Southport home.

"Bill is a good man, a grand companion and a great friend," says Philip Bollom. "He always thinks in terms of doing things for people, rather than to them, and that was why he was so highly regarded at all levels within the group and beyond. He always worked with zest and purpose, and by his enthusiasm, example and encouragement he drew the best out of the people around him."

Bill Davidson's brief had diversified so greatly during his later years with the group that it was important that various facets of his work were matched up with senior personnel best placed to take them up and develop them. For instance, he was group nominee on the board of Cleaning Tokens Ltd., and it was rightly felt that Richard Zerny, the managing director of Harris in Birmingham and a group board member, would be ideally suited to that role. Mr. Zerny has spent his entire career in the industry, from the age of 18 in 1962, and he came as an important "bonus" when the Hull-based family company founded by his grandfather and built up by his father and uncle joined the group in 1978. He became managing director of Zernys in 1979, after impressing Philip Bollom with his early work converting unit shops and adapting to the demands of textile rental, and in 1983 he moved on to the group board and the greater challenge of the Harris company, where he succeeded Terry Greer. "A very capable and conscientious director with a cutting edge," is Philip Bollom's view of Richard Zerny.

Bill Davidson's interests in trade associations were taken up with enthusiasm by Dennis Hargreaves, the managing director of James Hayes, and he made his mark so quickly that he was honoured with the presidency of the A.B.L.C.R.S. in 1988–'89. And as for industrial relations, personnel, education and training, the group took a further important step forward when it recruited Graham Gotts from the Littlewoods organisation to the newly-created and crucial post of group personnel officer. Mr. Gotts immediately embarked on an extensive series of management development training programmes from which several hundred employees, particularly such middle-ranking executives as retail district managers, have already benefited. There are often up to ten separate programmes in operation at Bootle at any one time, each one attended by a dozen staff members from throughout the group, and the personnel officer is fascinated by the prospect of identifying potential future executives at an early stage of their career. Topics covered range widely, managing and motivating, recruitment and interviewing, time-management, effective speaking and presentation, employment law and problem-solving and decision-making being typical examples, and the tutors are almost always experts from outside the company. "I see training and development as rather akin to the cost of maintaining plant and machinery," says Graham Gotts. "Both involve expenditure to bring the company's resources up to date and operating efficiently, whether those resources be human or mechanical." Philip Bollom certainly approves of his approach to the job. "Graham has a very professional and expert approach, and is achieving notable success," he says.

The end of 1987 brought the retirement of Brian Stapylton Thorley, managing director of Pullars since 1970 and a servant of the company for almost 36 years. When he first joined the famous old Perth firm in 1952 they were still a familiar name in almost every high street in Britain, and in 1953 Mr. Stapylton Thorley was appointed Lancashire area manager, serving branches not only in that county but in Cheshire, Cumberland and Northern Ireland. He was recalled to head office in 1956, rising from assistant sales manager to full sales managership in time for the takeover of the Rapid business and the opening of a satellite in Altrincham, and his first directorship in 1965 was well deserved. In 1972 he added to his responsibilities by becoming managing director of Stevenson's and the Arbroath Laundry, while in 1985 he joined the board of Johnson Micronclean. "I was impressed by Brian Thorley's sound commercial approach from the first time I met him," says Philip Bollom. "Like many people of my generation he lived for much of his life through a period of continuous change, and through it all he was always a strong and stable influence." His replacement at Pullars was Peter Robinson, a talented professional who had borne the brunt of Zernys' move into the textile rental field when he was Richard Zerny's No. 2 at Hull. For these efforts and much other good work he was rewarded with the managing directorship when Richard moved on to Harris, and now, like his former colleague, he had been given the chance to tread a larger stage. At Zernys he was in turn succeeded as M.D. by Vince Turton, a former service manager at Bootle and a man of wide experience of both retail and rental operations.

In March 1988 change was in the air at Jas. Smith and Sons at Dewsbury. Bob Binks stepped down after 26 years with the company, the final 20 of them as managing director, and in that time it had been consistently one of the most profitable in the group. The warm, genial son of a Durham miner, he came into dry cleaning after several working years spent variously as a gardener at a stately home, a member of RAF Transport Command and an industrial training officer, his first post being as personal assistant to Denis Smith, the chairman and grandson of the founder. By a strange irony, Mr. Denis died almost simultaneously with Bob Binks's retirement, at the age of 83 in Malvern, Worcestershire. In seeking a replacement managing director, the Johnson Group went for continuity in that it chose an executive who had been a member of the company for twenty years and a Smith director for four – but in a significant way it broke new ground, for the Lancashire-born Mrs. Josie Fairlie was the first woman to be promoted to such a position.

Philip Bollom has been sorry to see many other old colleagues depart over the years, among them Cyril Arnold, the popular Bollom company secretary who stepped down in 1979 after a long career that had also taken in Eastman and Lush and Cook; the Bollom brothers' cousin Donald Brooks, who took early retirement at the age of 55 in 1980, yet still managed to pack in 40 years' faithful work for the company, latterly as works director in Bristol and as the man responsible for unit shops in and around the city; and Jack Kneel, who in just five years with the group up to 1983 guided the integration into it of his old family firm, and later James Hayes. His speciality, and one of immense value to Johnson at that time, was textile rental, and the group's strengthening position in that field still owes much to his early influence.

All these and many others have left a void with their departure, but Philip Bollom is confident that the management team which he in turn leaves in 1989 is admirably equipped to face the challenges ahead. We have already met most members of the group board in these pages – James Fox, Richard Zerny, Arthur Winspear, Michael Sutton, John Mason, Jim Wahl from the U.S.A. – and the roll is completed by the contrasting personalities of Terry Greer and David Fowler. Managing director and Mr. Bollom's successor as chairman, Terry Greer came to Johnson from Sketchley as group marketing director in 1978, after more than two decades in retail dry cleaning. In October 1979 he moved to Birmingham as managing director of

Harris, a post he held until 1983, when he was appointed deputy group managing director. The managing director of that time, of course, was Philip Bollom, and Mr. Greer was promoted into the post he vacated when he became chairman in 1985. Much has happened in his relatively short time at Bootle, including the Nottingham bid, when he played a significant part in mustering institutional support for Johnson, and the take-off of the U.K. textile rental service. He sees the latter, and other forms of diversification in this country, as important areas of future growth. Like the majority of his board colleagues, he is convinced that the way ahead in dry cleaning, both in Britain and the States, is to operate through local names, the names by which the various Johnson companies are known and recognised in their own communities. "Dry cleaning is not a national image business, like chocolate or cigarettes," he says. "It's a multiple cottage industry, with customers coming in chiefly because the shop is convenient. If that's the case, and they get a welcome and a good service when they are there, that's all they want to know. Having worked for Sketchley for twenty years, where the one name stretched through the Midlands down to the South Coast, I know the single-name policy was correct for them because it had always been that way. They had grown under that name over a period of more than a hundred years, but essentially, if people used them it was not because they knew they had shops over half the country, but because they were the local cleaners. They were probably aware that they had branches in other local towns, but it really didn't make much difference. All I know is that the Johnson Group is extremely successful working in the way it does, and unless that position alters radically I see no need for change. If there has been a weakness in our diversified image in the past, it has been in trying to make people in the City aware of what the group really is. To them it must sometimes have appeared as an amorphous collection of different names, all a little difficult to grasp. but that isn't necessarily our problem. We have to make sure our eye is on the real ball all the time, and that is the dry cleaning customer. Apart from which, even the City is beginning to get to grips with us, after the hostile takeover bids and our great activity in America, particularly the acquisition of Dryclean USA.

"The strength Philip Bollom has brought to the group has been the sharp realisation of the need for an objective measurement of profit and of improvement, and a keen set of high standards of organisation. That was the message he preached as group managing director, and he hasn't stopped. It has been one of the reasons the group profit has improved so much. He is never satisfied with where we are currently – and that's an enormously strong driving force."

Philip Bollom recalls the fine job Terry Greer did as managing director of Harris and group marketing director before taking on the role of group managing director. "He is a sound and straightforward executive, and the group owes him a great debt of gratitude for the way in which he developed the textile rental business," says the outgoing chairman. "It really grew apace when he took it under his wing."

David Fowler has been in the industry since 1948, when he joined Martins the Cleaners. He has been a Johnson Group man since 1961, when he arrived at the age of 35 as inspector of branches, a post concerned chiefly with the development of unit shops. He was well qualified for such work, for as early as 1949 he had managed a Martin shop in Piccadilly, Manchester, which had boasted on-the-spot cleaning since before the war, and later in his career with the same company he set up more than 120 unit premises before moving to Johnson, which at that time had a mere handful. "When I came here it was a case of doing the whole thing all over again," he says. "I think I shall go down in history for opening more unit shops and closing more receiving offices than anyone else!" His efforts were rewarded by his appointment as managing director of Johnson Brothers from 1971, when he was also elevated to the group board.

Philip Bollom sees David Fowler as a down-to-earth man of common sense, the highest integrity and a strong social conscience. He is also, essentially, a people man in a people industry, well aware that the business is about more than dry cleaning solvents and balance sheets. "You find some very funny things in pockets," he says. "Some of them are extremely valuable, like rings and watches, others more plain embarrassing. When I was a manager in Piccadilly in Manchester, earning perhaps £10 a week, there was a bookie who would frequently leave rolls of £300 or £400 in notes in his pockets and not be aware of it – and not be at all surprised when you handed them back intact. It was in an interesting spot, that Piccadilly shop, then very much in the heart of it all at the top of Market Street. One of my best customers was a lady of the town who used to stand outside the old Queen's Hotel. She'd roll up with her cleaning every week in a taxi, a girl only about the same age as me, in her early twenties and very attractive. She'd always give me a pound tip, and I found that pretty attractive, too, but there was one time when I regretted the relationship. The owner of Martins used to come over once a month, and I would have dinner with him at the Queen's. One night we were coming out, and there she was in all her glory at the bottom of the steps. 'Hello, David,' she said, giving me a lovely smile, and I spent the rest of the evening explaining to him who was whose customer.

"Another time at Piccadilly we had the bright idea of setting up a little room at the back of the shop where we would press and spot clean gentlemen's trousers while they waited. One lunchtime someone came in obviously a little the worse for wear, and somehow we managed to stick him in this room and forget all about him. He must have gone to sleep, and it wasn't until six o'clock, just as I was preparing to lock up, that a little voice floated out of the back of the shop saying: 'You haven't forgotten me and my trousers, have you?'"

David Fowler retires in 1989 at much the same time as Philip Bollom. Bootle and the group will miss both of them, Philip Bollom for the reasons outlined through much of this book, and David Fowler for a host of admirable managerial qualities, of which a morale-boosting eye for the lighter moments of shop and factory life is just one.

17 – Greater than the Sum

As has been remarked throughout this book, one of the great strengths of the Johnson Group, and one of its most striking features, is its bringing together of a number of largely autonomous operating companies into a highly efficient and profitable whole. In Britain, the size of these companies varies considerably, from those with fewer than thirty shops to others with 100-plus, and their history is equally varied. Some, as we have seen, stem from pre-Victorian days, while several are strictly twentieth-century creations. And even in terms of being members of the group their pedigrees vary widely, for the world in which Jas. Smith and Son joined up in loose alliance with Johnson Bros. and Flinn and Son of Brighton in 1920 was a very different place from the one that saw the textile rental specialists James Hayes acquired under John Crockatt's chairmanship a few years ago.

In alphabetical order, leaving aside Bollom and Johnson Brothers, whose history has been treated at some length in earlier chapters, the first dry cleaning operating company on our list is John Crockatt Ltd., founded in Leeds by a 23-year-old Scot of that name in 1875. The product of a long apprenticeship in Perth, where his grandfather Peter Campbell had earlier married a Pullar widow, he was a colourful character. In the year before he set up in Leeds he walked from Brussels to Paris on hearing of a dyeing job, but by the time he reached Yorkshire for the second time – he had worked there briefly before his Continental exploits – he was still proclaiming his country of origin by wearing a Balmoral bonnet. He arrived at Leeds's Carlton Hill with £90 borrowed from his widowed mother, but as the three-storey warehouse and yard he had earmarked cost just £40 a year to rent, he was more than adequately provided for, and those premises stood him in good stead until 1908, when increased trade forced him to seek a larger factory at Stoney Rock Lane. He built his business from a staff of two, and though his wife bore four sons, two of whom became cleaners and dyers, they came along relatively late in his life, and were not able to make any significant contribution to the family firm until after the First World

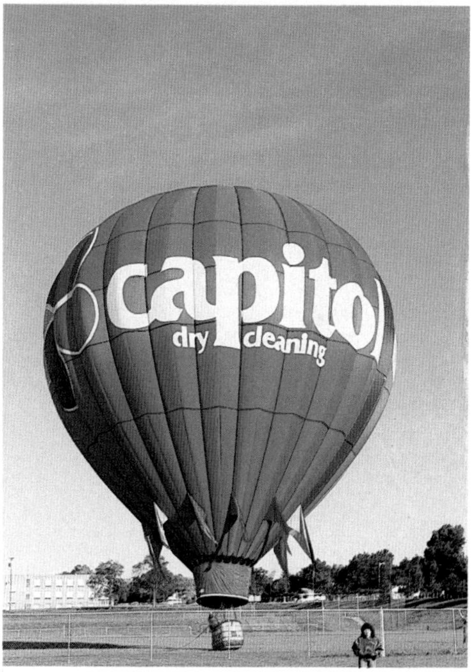

Selling yourself, U.S.-style: above, an Al Phillips outlet competing with the other bright lights of Las Vegas 24 hours a day, and right, the Capitol balloon that proclaims the company's name in the skies over Ohio.

Drive-through cleaning in the United States. A number of factors combine to keep such outlets to the minimum in Britain.

Setting the pace in Britain: a Pullars outlet in an Asda superstore at Portlethen, near Aberdeen, and a rare British drive-in in Smiths' Yorkshire territory, far away from the Nevada sun.

'Is that the whole tanker full?'

'It's all in there, Sir.'

'Splendid,' the Baron said. 'Blud, pass me the matches. It's time to smoke out the trolls.'

Blud fumbled in his jacket pocket and handed Baron Marackai a crumpled box of matches.

Baron Marackai struck a match and its flame fizzed, then went out. He tried to strike another but it snapped in two. 'These are old matches, Blud!'

'I found them on the reception desk at the hotel,' Blud told him.

'You useless fool,' Baron Marackai muttered. He took the remaining matches from the box and struck them all at once. They sputtered into flame and he dropped them down the hole. There was a whooshing sound as the oil caught fire and flames roared underground. All across the snowy mountain, thick black smoke began billowing from holes and caves.

'Get ready!' Baron Marackai ordered. He hid behind Bone, using the big man as a human shield. Blud crouched beside him.

'Not you, Blud,' Baron Marackai said. 'You're the shooter!' He pushed the small man into the open.

Blud stood shivering in the wind and snow, his eyes darting from left to right as he pointed his rifle from one smoking cave to another.

From inside the mountain came the sounds of underground beasts: growls and squeals, bellows and squawks. Beasts came hurrying from caves, trying to escape the smoke. An ice-bear bounded out into the snow, roaring. A vampire owl flew screeching into the air. A giant wraith spider scurried out, hissing.

'It's the trolls I want!' the Baron shouted.

'There's one!' Bone called.

From a smoking cave, a huge green troll charged out on all fours, swiping the air with its long tusks. It roared, snorting smoke from its nostrils. The troll saw Blud and stood tall, beating its chest. 'Oof! Oof! Oof!'

'Help!' Blud cried.

Baron Marackai peered out from behind Bone, pointing. 'Shoot it, you moron!'

Blud aimed his rifle at the troll. His teeth rattled as he squeezed the trigger and fired. A feathered tranquillizer dart shot out and struck the troll on the chest.

The troll stumbled, then toppled to the ground with a thud. It lay in the snow, face down, unconscious.

Blud spun round as another big green troll ran from the mouth of a cave.

'Aim between its eyes!' the Baron shouted.

Blud fired another tranquillizer dart, hitting the troll on the arm. It tumbled into the snow. Another troll burst out and Blud fired again. The feathered dart hit the troll on the nose.

'Behind you!' Bone called.

Two more trolls charged out from the smoke-filled mountain and Blud fired twice. The trolls fell, one on top of the other.

Troll after troll burst from the caves. There was oofing and roaring, and the whizz and crack of tranquillizer darts firing from the rifle. One by one they toppled into the snow.

Slowly, the mountain fell silent and the

smoke began to clear. More than twenty trolls lay tranquillized and unconscious on the ground.

'Splendid!' Baron Marackai said, stepping out from behind Bone.

He walked through the snow to one of the trolls and kicked it with his serpent-skin boot. 'Sleeping like a baby,' he said. 'Bone, pick out five young ones and load them on to the cattle truck.'

Bone trudged over to inspect the tranquillized trolls. 'How do I tell which are the young ones, Sir? They all look big and ugly.'

'The young ones have the softest skin,' Baron Marackai told him.

Bone knelt down and pinched a troll's cheek, tugging its thick rubbery skin.

Blud skittered over to the Baron. 'What are we going to do with them, Sir?' he asked.

The Baron rubbed his hands together. 'We shall use them in the Predatron,' he said.

'The Predatron!' Blud said excitedly. 'These stupid beasts won't stand a chance.'

'But what if we get caught, Sir?' Blud asked. The small man glanced shiftily from side to side. 'What if you-know-who find out?'

'I have prepared for that,' Baron Marackai said, grinning.

The Baron stroked the small stump of flesh on his right hand where his little finger was missing. He held his hand up. 'Now, repeat after me. Death to the RSPCB!'

Blud and Bone turned down their little fingers then held up their right hands. 'Death to the RSCPC!' they said.

'The RS*PCB*, you numbskulls!'

The Baron picked up two handfuls of snow and pushed them in the men's faces. 'Now load those trolls on the truck! I have important business to attend to.'

Blud and Bone wiped the snow from their eyes and watched curiously as the Baron strode off across the mountain. He was peering into the caves.

'Where are you?' the Baron called. 'Come to Marackai.'

He glanced over at a small hole about twenty metres away. The head of a creature with pointy ears and large white eyes was poking from it.

The Baron waved. 'Coo-ee!'

The creature ducked as Baron Marackai ran towards it.

The Baron reached into the hole and pulled the creature out by its neck. 'Well, well, what have we here?' he said, screwing up his nose.

It was a little grey goblin. It was dirty and wrinkly and wriggled in the Baron's grasp. In its bony hand the goblin was clutching a small black bat.

'Don't hurt me,' the goblin pleaded, its fat snout twitching.

The Baron smiled, his face twisting like a rotten apple core. 'Spying are you, goblin?'

The goblin's white eyes blinked. 'Help!' it called.

'There's no one to help you here, you revolting little creature,' the Baron said. 'The RSPCB is miles away!'

The goblin looked down at its bat. 'What to do, little bat? What to do?' he muttered.

'Give that to me, goblin,' Baron Marackai ordered.

'No! Not my bat!'

The Baron reached for the bat in the goblin's hands. 'I SAID, GIVE IT TO ME!'

CHAPTER TWO

At the RSPCB, the Royal Society for the Prevention of Cruelty to Beasts, Ulf was riding his quad bike through the beast park. The sun was shining as he sped across the Great Grazing Grounds then up on to the bridge above the meat-eaters' enclosures. Beneath him, in brick-walled pens, carnivorous beasts looked up: a gorgon hissed, a long-haired minotaur snorted at him and an Egyptian scorpius rattled its tail.

Halfway along the bridge, Ulf stopped and looked over at a beast with the body of a giraffe and the head of a piranha. This was the giranha, the tallest of all the meat-eaters. Its head was as high as the bridge. It turned towards Ulf, gnashing its teeth.

Ulf reached into a feeding-sack on the back of his quad bike and picked out a frozen chicken. 'Lunchtime,' he called, throwing the chicken across to the giranha.

The beast lunged with its long neck and snapped the chicken out of the air. Ulf watched as it gobbled the chicken whole.

'You're going home today,' he told it. 'Orson's coming to fetch you.'

Ulf turned, hearing the trees part at the edge of the Dark Forest. Orson the giant came striding out with a thick rope looped over his shoulder. 'How is she?' the giant boomed.

'She's doing fine,' Ulf called.

Orson strode to the gate of the giranha's enclosure and slid its metal bolt. As the giant pulled the gate open, the giranha reared up on its hind legs. 'Woah there!' Orson said.

The giranha stomped its hooves into the ground, gouging out great chunks of earth. It started screeching.

'Easy girl,' Orson said, clipping a beast collar to the end of his rope. The giranha lunged for him with open jaws, and Orson clicked the collar around the beast's neck. He heaved on the rope with his powerful arms, bringing the giranha under control.

Orson was huge. He could handle any beast. He looked at Ulf on the bridge. 'Off you go.'

Ulf revved his bike engine, then rode down the end of the bridge waving another frozen chicken in the air. 'Here girl, come and get it,' he called.

The giranha swung its head round to watch him.

'That's it, Ulf,' Orson said. 'Now let her have it!'

Ulf threw the chicken into the air. Orson relaxed the rope and the giranha lunged from its enclosure, catching the chicken in its jaws.

Ulf held a third chicken over his head as he rode into the Dark Forest. 'Come and get your food,' he called.

He sped along the forest track and heard the

giranha stomping behind him, pushing through the trees. He threw the chicken over his head, then glanced back to see the beast snap the frozen bird from the branches. Orson gripped the rope tightly, stopping the giranha from charging. Ulf held up a fourth chicken and accelerated away, luring the beast through the forest.

A sparkle flew across the track in front of him. It was Tiana the fairy. 'Hello, Ulf,' she said.

'Mind out, Tiana,' Ulf called, swerving. 'The giranha's coming!'

Tiana was Ulf's friend and lived in the Dark Forest with the other fairies. She was gathering leaves to make an autumn cloak.

She darted behind a tree and peered out nervously as the giranha stomped past, spitting out chicken bones.

Ulf rode on round the swamp and through the bracken. He jumped his bike over fallen branches and skidded on wet leaves. He splashed through puddles, and mud flew up

from the quad bike's wheels, splattering his jeans and T-shirt. Then the trees thinned and he rode out into the afternoon sun. He heard the screech of the giranha as it came out of the forest behind him, followed by Orson.

The giant called to him: 'Tell Dr Fielding the giranha's ready to go!'

The RSPCB was a rescue centre for rare and endangered beasts. The giranha had been brought in three months earlier, suffering from a broken hind leg. Dr Fielding, the RSPCB vet, had inserted a metre-long metal rod into its thigh bone to mend it. Orson had helped the giranha get strong again by taking it swimming in the freshwater lake. Now it was fully recovered and ready to be released back into the wild.

Ulf sped along the edge of the freshwater lake and into the paddock. The jackalopes were leaping in the sunshine. He heard a griffin screech from the aviary and looked across to see it landing in the branches of an oak tree. Ulf placed his hairy feet onto the foot bars and stood up on his quad bike, twisting back the bike's throttle with his hairy hand.

Though he looked like a human boy, Ulf was *beast blood*. He was a werewolf, a morphing beast, and on the full moon he would change from boy to wolf. The RSPCB was his home.

'Open,' he called as he reached a gate at the top of the paddock. The voice-activated gate opened automatically and he rode into the yard, pulling up outside a large country mansion. This was Farraway Hall, the headquarters of the RSPCB. Ulf stood up on his bike seat and peered in an open window. 'Dr Fielding,' he called.

'One moment, Ulf.'

He could see Dr Fielding in her office. She was on the telephone, speaking into the handset: 'That's terrific news, Minister. Antarctic dragons are the only flightless dragons in existence. A preservation order is long overdue. Thank you.'

She put the phone down. 'What is it, Ulf?'

'Orson's bringing the giranha in,' Ulf told her.

'Excellent. The transporter's waiting. I'll meet you out the front.'

Ulf rode round to the forecourt at the front of Farraway Hall. Parked by the entrance gates was the tallest lorry he'd ever seen. Its back doors were open and a ramp led up inside. It had straw on the floor and a trough of water.

He heard the stomping of hooves coming round the side of the house. He looked back and saw the giranha, being held by Orson. 'Easy girl,' the giant said.

Ulf threw four frozen chickens into the back of the lorry. The giranha saw them and stomped up the ramp. It screeched, then snapped one of them from the straw.

'That's it, big friend,' Orson said to the beast. 'Eat it up.'

While the giranha munched the chicken, Orson attached harnessing straps around its body to keep it steady on the long journey ahead. He stepped down and closed the doors. 'Thanks, Ulf,' he said.

Dr Fielding came out from the house and went over to the lorry to speak to the driver in his cab. 'Look after her,' she said. 'She's a soppy old thing really.'

'I'll see she makes it back safely,' the driver replied, starting the lorry's engine.

Ulf jumped off his quad bike and opened the front gates. He watched as the lorry drove out, heading away up the long driveway. The giranha was going back to its home in the African jungle. Ulf felt glad. He imagined it roaming free, pushing through the jungle trees.

'Well done, everyone,' Dr Fielding said, as she bolted the gates shut. 'One giranha safely mended and returning to the wild.'

Ulf smiled then hopped back on to his quad bike and rode after Orson. The giant was striding across the yard, whistling. 'Do you need a hand with anything else?' Ulf asked.

'No thanks, Ulf. I've just got to give the sandwhale its scrub, then I'm done,' Orson said. He picked up a broom from beside the kit room and slipped it into his belt. 'You get yourself something to eat, Ulf,' the giant told him. 'You need to be strong for tomorrow.'

Tomorrow night Ulf's transformation would take place. The moon would be full and he'd change from boy to wolf.

While Orson headed towards the desert dome, Ulf parked his bike by the feedstore. He fetched a sausage from the meat fridge, and sat on the paddock gate, eating it. The Mexican jackalopes were leaping in the long grass. He heard the low bellow of the Mongolian armourpod from out on the Great Grazing Grounds, and from Sunset Mountain came the *hurroooooo* of Bigfoot.

All the beasts would one day leave and go back to their homes in the wild, he thought. Ulf wondered when it would be his turn. He'd lived at the RSPCB almost all his life, ever since he'd been brought in as a werecub.

Ulf saw a sparkle shooting high over the paddock. It was Tiana the fairy.

'Look, Ulf,' she called, pointing. She was flying towards Farraway Hall, following a little black bat.

'A messenger bat!' Ulf said, excitedly. He jumped off the gate and ran towards the house, watching the bat circle above the chimney pots. It perched on the nose of a stone gargoyle that was leaning from the rooftop.

Uh-oh, Ulf thought.

The gargoyle turned from stone to flesh. It reached up. 'Gotcha!' it said, cupping its hands around the little black bat.

'Leave it alone, Druce!' Tiana yelled.

Druce the gargoyle stuck his yellow tongue out at the fairy then scuttled down a drainpipe, clutching the bat.

'Drop it, Druce!' Ulf said, running over. 'It's a messenger bat.'

'Messagy bat,' Druce gurgled, jumping to the ground. 'Drucey caught it.' The gargoyle held the bat close to his chest and pulled an ugly face.

Just then, the side door of Farraway Hall

opened and Dr Fielding came out. 'What's all the noise?'

'A messenger bat's come in,' Ulf explained.

Dr Fielding looked at the gargoyle. 'Druce, give that to me,' she said.

The gargoyle's mouth drooped.

'Be good, Druce,' she warned, stepping over to him.

Druce opened his hands and Dr Fielding took the small black bat. 'Thank you.'

'Blurgh!' Druce replied, blowing a raspberry, then he scurried back up the drainpipe to the roof.

'Who's it from?' Ulf asked.

Dr Fielding held the bat, inspecting a small gold ring on its leg. Engraved on the ring was a code. 'Spotter NOR8,' Dr Fielding read.

Tucked into the ring was a scrap of paper. 'Ulf, could you check the message, please?'

While Dr Fielding held the bat, Ulf carefully pulled out the scrap of paper from the ring. He unrolled it. Scrawled on it was a single word: HELP!

HELP!

CHAPTER THREE

'Who's spotter NOR8?' Ulf asked, following Dr Fielding as she carried the messenger bat into Farraway Hall.

'I'll have to check the spotters' database,' Dr Fielding said.

Spotters were voluntary members of the RSPCB stationed around the world. They were essential to the RSPCB's global operations, relaying data on beast activity in the wild.

Dr Fielding was hurrying down the corridor. Ulf ran after her, holding the message in his hand. 'Do you think it's an emergency?' he asked. All the message said was HELP!

'Hopefully it's nothing serious,' Dr Fielding replied, opening the door of the data room.

Ulf stuffed the message in his pocket as he went inside.

The data room was the hub of the RSPCB Spotter Network. Pinned to the walls were maps and letters, and photographs of beasts. There was a spotters' board where beast sightings were recorded, shelves stacked with reports, and a desk with a computer and a small bat-cage beside it.

Dr Fielding placed the messenger bat in the cage, then sat at the computer to check the spotters' database. She tapped in the code NOR8 and the computer began searching.

Ulf saw Tiana waving at the window. He opened it and she flew in and landed by the bat-cage.

'I'll feed it,' she said. With both hands the fairy prised the lid from a tin marked MESSENGER MEALS. She picked out a dried grasshopper and poked it through the bars of the cage.

While the bat nibbled, Ulf looked at the spotters' board, reading the spotter codes on recent beast sightings from around the world:

SPOTTER AUS129: Mermaid spotted in Sydney harbour, Australia.

SPOTTER GBR215: Demon sighted at Westminster Cathedral, England.

SPOTTER USA333: Nixies found nesting in cornfield in Delaware, Pennsylvania. First of the season!

SPOTTER NEP56: Yeti footprints seen near food stores at Mount Everest base-camp.

'That's odd,' Dr Fielding said.

Ulf turned to the computer screen. It said **SPOTTER INACTIVE**.

'It must be one of the old ones,' Dr Fielding said. She span her chair to face the door, then put her fingers in her mouth and whistled. A small hand-shaped beast came scuttling on its fingertips into the room. It ran up the leg of her desk and tapped its finger, awaiting instructions. It was the Helping Hand, a busy beast that helped Dr Fielding with the RSPCB paperwork. 'Can you see what we've got on NOR8?' Dr Fielding asked it.

The Helping Hand scuttled to a cupboard in the corner. It pulled open the door with its fingers, and bundles of paper fell out on to the floor. The cupboard was stuffed full. The Helping Hand began rifling through folders and notes. Ulf watched as it pulled out sheets of paper, tossing them to the side. Then it disappeared to the back of the cupboard and Ulf heard rustling. The Helping Hand was leafing through the very oldest of the spotter files – spotters who had not been in contact with the RSPCB since the database was computerized.

'Most of the older spotters are inactive now,' Dr Fielding explained.

The Helping Hand came scurrying out holding a tatty sheet of paper. It climbed on to the table and handed the paper to Dr Fielding.

'Thank you,' she said.

Ulf looked. She was holding a form, creased and yellowed with age, and filled in by hand with black ink. On the top of the form it said

RSPCB SPOTTER LICENCE and in the upper corner was the code NOR8. Stapled to the form was a black-and-white photograph.

'How peculiar,' Dr Fielding said. She showed the photograph to Ulf. It was of a beast with large white eyes, pointy ears and a fat snout. 'Spotter NOR8 is a goblin,' she said.

'A goblin!' Tiana cried, looking up from the bat-cage.

'What's strange about that?' Ulf asked.

'I've not heard of a goblin being a spotter before,' Dr Fielding told him. She read the form. 'Name: Gumball.'

'Goblins are revolting, Ulf,' Tiana said. 'They're dirty and smelly. And they steal things.'

Dr Fielding frowned at the fairy. 'Tiana, that's not nice.'

'Well, it's true,' the fairy said. 'Goblins shouldn't be allowed to be spotters.'

Dr Fielding continued reading. 'Stationed in Norway.'

'Norway?' Ulf asked.

'A place called Honeycomb Mountain.

That messenger bat's flown all the way across the sea.'

Dr Fielding typed **Honeycomb Mountain** into her computer, pulling up information from the database. 'Honeycomb Mountain is in the Jotunheim Range.'

A three-dimensional digital image of a mountain came up on the computer screen. It was riddled with holes and caves and a network of tunnels.

'It's a habitat for underground beasts,' she said.

Dr Fielding clicked on images of wraith spiders, elephant leeches, cave mantises, sword serpents and longtusk trolls.

'What do you think's happened there?' Ulf asked.

'I expect the goblin's just got stuck in a hole,' she said.

'Goblins are always poking their noses into places they're not meant to,' Tiana added.

Ulf watched as Dr Fielding plugged in a handheld GPRS tracker and downloaded the information from the computer.

'You're not *going* there, are you?' Tiana asked. 'It's only a goblin.'

'Even so, I should check it out,' Dr Fielding said. 'I'll take the helicopter.'

She pulled up a satellite map on the computer screen to check the weather. It was swirling with dark cloud. 'There's a storm over the ocean. It's blowing this way,' she said. 'I'll leave first thing in the morning, as soon as the sky's clear.'

'Can I come with you?' Ulf asked her. He'd never met a goblin before. Despite what Tiana had said, he thought he'd quite like to.

'It's okay, Orson will come with me,' Dr Fielding told him. She got up and stepped to the door. 'We won't be gone long.'

'But I might be able to help,' Ulf said.

'The wild's a dangerous place, Ulf,' Dr Fielding told him. 'Anyway, I need you to look after things here.' She left the room and headed off down the corridor.

Ulf felt disappointed. He never got to go on expeditions.

'Who on earth would make a goblin a spotter?' Tiana muttered. She was stroking the bat through the bars of the cage.

Ulf looked down at the Spotter Licence. He read the RSPCB oath printed on it:

"I do solemnly swear to preserve and protect the wild. From this day forth, I pledge my allegiance to beasts."

Under the oath was a signature scrawled in awkward handwriting:

Gumball

Below it was written:

Appointed by Professor J.E. Farraway

'It was Professor Farraway,' Ulf said. 'Professor Farraway made the goblin a spotter.'

'He must have been crazy,' Tiana muttered.

Ulf frowned at her.

Professor Farraway had lived at Farraway Hall a long time ago. He'd been the world's first cryptozoologist and the founder of the RSPCB.

Just then, Ulf heard moanings and groanings coming from upstairs. He rushed to the door of the data room and poked his head out.

'Where are you going?' Tiana asked.

'Listen. It's him, Tiana,' Ulf said. Professor Farraway's ghost now haunted the old library at Farraway Hall. 'Let's see what he wants.'

Ulf started running down the corridor to the staircase.

'But it's spooky up there,' Tiana called, flying after him. Ulf was climbing the stairs. 'Come back, Ulf,' she said.

Ulf looked down. The little fairy was perched on the banister. Her wing tips were quivering. 'You're not frightened are you?' Ulf asked.

'Of course I'm not,' the fairy replied, crossing her arms.

Ulf reached his hand down to her. 'Come on. There's nothing to be afraid of.'

Tiana held tightly to the hairs on Ulf's palm. 'Just promise me we'll stick together,' she said.

CHAPTER FOUR

Ulf headed up the stairs with Tiana in his hand. He crept along the Gallery of Science and through the Room of Curiosities, past RSPCB artefacts and equipment from early expeditions. He stopped at a door on the far wall, the entrance to the old library where the non-corporeal beasts lived: ghosts, ghouls and spectres. Moanings and groanings were coming from inside. 'Ready?' he asked Tiana.

But before she could reply, the door creaked open. In the gloom of the library, Ulf saw a glowing blue mist disappearing through cracks between the floorboards. In the corner of the room a screaming mouth vanished into the wall, and on the upper reading level three ghostly grey heads rose up through the ceiling.

Ulf could feel Tiana clinging to his finger as the moanings and groanings fell silent. From the darkness on the far side of the library, Ulf saw a candle floating towards him. Its flame was flickering, lighting up the bookshelves.

'Professor, is that you?' he asked.

The candle drifted past Ulf's side and he felt a cold chill as the Professor's ghost went straight through him.

'Where's he going?' Tiana whispered.

The candle floated out through the doorway into the Room of Curiosities, hovering over boxes and crates.

'Professor, come back,' Ulf called, stepping after him.

The candle weaved between glass cabinets and cases. It floated past a dragon's tethering chain on the wall, and the chain began rattling. It hovered over a jar of vampire teeth, and the teeth began chattering.

'What's he up to?' Tiana asked.

The candle was lighting up objects, drifting over tables and along display cabinets. The lids of trunks and chests opened and closed. Drawers slid out and cupboard doors swung open.

'I don't know,' Ulf said.

The candle drifted to the far corner of the room and settled on a table. From beneath the table an old canvas rucksack slid out.

Ulf stepped over to it and saw its straps unbuckling. Objects rose out of the rucksack: a shiny silver compass flew out and popped into Ulf's pocket; a climbing rope snaked up and coiled around his shoulder; a metal head torch floated up and strapped itself to his head.

'Professor, what are you doing?' Ulf asked.

Tiana looked at Ulf, giggling. 'You look like an explorer.'

Ulf watched as an old map floated from a pouch in the rucksack and unfolded in the air. The map was drawn by hand in black ink, and was stained and streaked with dirt. It showed underground tunnels. Ulf could see passages connecting caves and caverns. They were labelled in tiny handwriting: *Spider's Larder, Troll Chamber, Leech Lair, Gumball's Grotto.*

'Tiana, look!' he said. 'This is where the goblin's stationed.'

At the bottom of the map it said *Honeycomb Mountain.*

The map folded itself up, then drifted down and wedged into Ulf's pocket.

'Let's get out of here,' Tiana said, flying past the candle. 'This is creepy.'

'Wait a minute,' Ulf said. He could hear something rattling in the rucksack. The strap on its side pocket undid and a small red box floated out.

Ulf took hold of the box. Its lid opened and inside it he saw bullets.

He gasped.

'Put that down, Ulf!' Tiana cried.

Ulf dropped the box and it landed with a clatter, the bullets spilling out across the floor.

'Let's go now,' Tiana told him. 'Bullets are dangerous.'

But as Ulf began edging away, he felt the icy chill of the Professor's ghost sweep through him. The hairs on Ulf's neck stood on end. He looked down. The bullets were moving on the floor, rolling out from under tables and behind crates. They were sliding back into the box. The box lid closed and it floated back up into his hand.

'Put that down, Ulf,' Tiana pleaded.

'But I can't, Tiana. He won't let me.'

The box of bullets was being pressed into Ulf's palm. On its side he saw the words: **TITANIUM-TIPPED BEAST BULLETS**.

The candle flickered and went out.

CHAPTER FIVE

Ulf ran out of the Room of Curiosities and along the Gallery of Science. As he passed a picture on the wall, he caught a glimpse of his reflection in the glass. He stopped, seeing the rope around his shoulder and the head torch strapped to his head. He stared at the box of bullets in his hand.

'You should give those to Dr Fielding,' Tiana said, hovering in front of him.

'But what was the Professor doing, Tiana?'

The fairy tugged on Ulf's ear. 'He was just being spooky,' she said, flying to the staircase. 'Come on.'

Ulf followed the fairy downstairs and into

the yard. He saw Dr Fielding and Orson by the kit room, getting ready for their expedition to Honeycomb Mountain. The sun was starting to go down and dark clouds were blowing in from the sea.

'The storm's coming,' Tiana said, hovering in front of Ulf.

Ulf hardly noticed her. He was still thinking about what the Professor had shown him.

'Go on, give Dr Fielding those bullets,' Tiana said.

A cold gust of wind blew the fairy head over heels and she grabbed Ulf's T-shirt to steady herself. 'I'm going back to the forest.'

Tiana started flying across the yard, weaving in the wind. 'I'll see you in the morning,' she called, then she disappeared over the big beast barn.

Ulf ran to Dr Fielding, clutching the box of bullets.

'Where have you been, Ulf?' Dr Fielding asked, seeing him dressed like an explorer.

'In the Room of Curiosities,' Ulf told her.

Orson bent down to look at the rope around Ulf's shoulder and the head torch on his head. 'Been rummaging through the Professor's things, have you?'

The giant tapped the metal head torch with his finger. 'They don't make them like that any more.'

'I found these,' Ulf said, showing Dr Fielding the box of bullets.

Dr Fielding took the box from him. 'Ulf, what are you doing with bullets?' she asked.

'They were with the Professor's things,' Ulf explained.

She took a bullet from the box and inspected it closely. 'This is live ammunition, Ulf. It's extremely dangerous.'

The bullet was shiny and its tip was sharpened to a point.

'Why would the Professor have bullets?' Ulf asked her.

Dr Fielding furrowed her brow. 'I think he probably confiscated these from a beast hunt. They're beast-hunting bullets, Ulf.'

Orson knelt down to take a look. 'Nasty things,' he said. 'Only humans could invent something so horrible.'

'Humans?' Ulf asked.

'They used to hunt beasts for sport, Ulf,' the giant said. 'They used to—'

'Orson, that's enough,' Dr Fielding interrupted. She turned to Ulf. 'There are no beast hunts any more, Ulf. Professor Farraway helped pass a law many years ago making them illegal. It was a major victory for beast protection.'

Ulf watched as Dr Fielding put the box of bullets in her pocket. 'I shall destroy these at once,' she told him. 'And if you ever find anything like these again, don't touch them, just come and tell me.'

Dr Fielding gave Ulf a stern look, then headed back across the yard to the house.

Ulf saw Druce the gargoyle leering from the roof of Farraway Hall. The gargoyle stared down at Dr Fielding and pointed his fingers like a gun. 'Bang!' he called. 'Bang! Bang!'

Dr Fielding looked up and saw Druce giggling. 'That's not funny, Druce,' she said.

The gargoyle pulled an ugly face, then turned to stone as Dr Fielding opened the side door of Farraway Hall. She glanced back at Orson. 'We'll leave at dawn,' she called. 'You'll need your flying cable.' The giant gave a thumbs-up and Dr Fielding headed inside.

'I think she's cross with me,' Ulf said.

'No she's not, Ulf. She just worries about you,' Orson told him.

The giant opened the kit room door and reached in, gathering the kit for the expedition.

'Those bullets were with the Professor's things from Honeycomb Mountain,' Ulf said.

'I expect they got put up there by accident,' Orson replied. 'The Room of Curiosities is packed with old stuff from all over the place.'

Orson pulled out his flying cable. He was too big to fit in the helicopter so he flew beneath it, suspended on a long steel cable with a footstrap at its end. He reached in again and pulled out a huge vest made from woven metal.

'What's that?' Ulf asked, staring at it.

'It's my chainmail vest,' Orson replied. 'In case of trolls.' He held it up for Ulf to see. The metal was worn and dented. 'Dr Fielding says there are longtusk trolls at Honeycomb Mountain. They're the biggest trolls of all, Ulf. Their tusks can go right through you.'

Orson folded the vest, then reached in for Dr Fielding's rucksack and caving boots.

'Do you think something bad has happened at Honeycomb Mountain?' Ulf asked.

The giant stood up, holding the kit in his arms. 'Don't pay too much attention to what a goblin says, Ulf. They're always causing trouble. The last time I saw one, it was stealing my kettle.' He gave Ulf a wink, then strode off across the yard towards the helicopter. As he reached the forecourt he turned. 'Don't worry about a thing, Ulf,' he called. 'We'll be back before you know it.'

Ulf looked up at the evening sky.

Stormclouds were gathering overhead.

CHAPTER SIX

As the sky darkened, Ulf headed down the side of the big beast barn towards a stone hut with bars on its window. This was his den. He stepped inside, taking the rope from his shoulder, then pulled off the head torch and took the map and compass from his pockets. The message from Gumball the spotter fell out in the straw and he sat down looking at it: HELP! he read.

Ulf was wondering what had happened to the goblin. No one seemed to like goblins very much. No one except Professor Farraway, anyway. He reached to the back of his den and from his secret hiding place took out a small black book. It was Professor Farraway's old notebook: *The Book of Beasts*. He began flicking through the pages, past jottings on tracking pixies and a step-by-step guide to demon dentistry. He saw a sketch of the boola monster, a diagram of a minotaur's skull and tips on how to bottle a poltergeist. He found a section on underground beasts and stopped at an entry headed GOBLINS. Ulf read:

Goblins are expert thieves. They watch from the shadows, waiting to steal a scrap of meat or a shiny jewel to brighten their caves. Nothing goes on underground that a goblin doesn't see. Considered dirty and untrustworthy, they are seldom liked, but be nice to a goblin and it will help you, for a goblin will never forget a friend.

Ulf felt the wind blowing through the bars of his window. It was dark outside and starting to rain. He gathered the Professor's things around him, and tucked his knees into his chest. He imagined the Professor long ago on his expedition to Honeycomb Mountain, exploring the tunnels and caves underground. Then he thought about the bullets in the rucksack. Why did the Professor give them to him?

Ulf heard a gurgling sound and the patter of feet scurrying across the roof of his den. The sky flashed with lightning, and he saw Druce's face appear upside-down at the door.

The gargoyle pointed his fingers at Ulf. 'Bang!'

Ulf jumped. 'What are you doing here, Druce?'

The gargoyle dropped down and scurried around the side of Ulf's den. 'Drucey goes a-hunting. Hunting little beasties,' Ulf heard him gurgle.

The gargoyle popped up at the window, grinning. He pointed his fingers through the bars. 'Bang! Bang!'

'Stop mucking about, Druce,' Ulf said.

Druce blew the end of his fingers like a gun. He leant in further, screwing up his ugly face. '*Ma-rrrrackai* hunted beasts.'

'What are you talking about, Druce?' Ulf asked. Hearing the name Marackai sent a chill down Ulf's spine.

'Bad Marackai,' Druce said.

The gargoyle put his little finger into his mouth and bit it. 'I bited him,' he said. 'I bited his finger off.'

The gargoyle giggled, then ran off, bounding through the rain back to Farraway Hall. Ulf could see him scampering up to the dark rooftop. The gargoyle was singing: 'He comes in the night with his gun and his knife. Run away, Fur Face, run for your life!'

Ulf lay down in the darkness, thinking about Marackai. Marackai was Professor Farraway's son and had once lived at Farraway Hall. He hated beasts, and had been vicious and cruel to them. He'd been sent away, but twice he'd tried to take Farraway Hall back for himself. Twice Ulf had defeated him.

Ulf tried to sleep, but he couldn't. He had a creepy feeling that something bad was happening at Honeycomb Mountain. He stayed awake all night listening to the storm, thinking about the message and the bullets. As the storm blew itself out and the first rays of dawn appeared in the sky, Ulf knew what he had to do. He had to go on the expedition. He had to find out what was wrong.

Ulf picked up the head torch from the straw and put it on. He stuffed the map and compass into his pockets and slung the rope over his shoulder, then he crept out of his den.

The rain had stopped and the clouds were clearing. In the half-light, he saw Orson's lantern glowing from across the beast park. The giant was on his way back from giving the beasts their early-morning feed. Ulf ran through the yard to the corner of the house and saw Dr Fielding loading her medical rucksack into the back of the helicopter.

He looked up at Druce asleep on the rooftop. 'Psst,' he said.

The gargoyle turned from stone to flesh as he woke up.

'Keep an eye on things here for me, Druce,' Ulf whispered.

The gargoyle scurried down the drainpipe. 'Where's Fur Face going?' he gurgled.

'To Honeycomb Mountain,' Ulf whispered. 'You're in charge now.'

Druce smiled. 'Drucey the boss!'

'Ssh,' Ulf said. He saw Dr Fielding climbing into the cockpit of the helicopter. She was checking the flight controls.

Ulf saw that the cargo hold was open. With no one looking, he dashed across the forecourt and jumped into the back of the helicopter. He scrambled behind the pile of kit.

'Ready to go!' Dr Fielding called.

Ulf heard Orson's footsteps coming round the side of the house. He stayed hidden behind the kit as the giant loaded a lantern into the back of the helicopter. The door slid shut. It was pitch dark in the cargo hold. Ulf switched on his head torch and the light shone on metal walls. There were no windows. Then from under Orson's chainmail vest, a sparkle flew out. It was Tiana the fairy.

'Tiana!' Ulf said, amazed. 'What are you doing here?'

Tiana hovered in the torchlight. She was wearing a warm red cloak made from a pleated sycamore leaf. 'You didn't think I'd let you go on an expedition without me, did you?'

'But how did you know I was coming?'

Tiana smiled. 'You're a werewolf. You're always up to something.'

Ulf heard Dr Fielding calling to Orson outside. Then suddenly the helicopter engine started and Ulf heard the blades beginning to turn. He felt the helicopter lift off the ground.

'We're off,' he said excitedly.

There was a clanking sound as Orson clipped his flying cable to the bottom of the helicopter, then a jolt as the giant was lifted into the air.

Ulf felt the helicopter surge forwards, carrying him away from Farraway Hall.

CHAPTER SEVEN

Baron Marackai stood behind the reception desk in an old hotel, counting a bundle of money. He looked up as the front door opened and a flurry of snowflakes blew into the lobby. A man stepped inside, dragging a suitcase. He was wearing a camouflage jacket and a cowboy hat. He stamped his snowy boots on the mat.

'Ah, Mr Armstrong,' the Baron said. 'Welcome to Loadem Lodge.'

'Howdy,' the man replied.

'You're just in time for morning coffee. The others are waiting. If you wouldn't mind paying in advance, I'll show you through.'

'How much does this thing cost?' the man asked, pulling a wad of bank notes from his pocket.

The Baron took *all* the money. 'That'll do nicely,' he said. Then he rang a little bell on the desk and Bone came lumbering into the lobby, wearing a small peaked cap.

'My porter will take your bags upstairs, Mr Armstrong,' Baron Marackai said. He handed Bone a key attached to a key-ring in the shape of a pistol. 'Room five,' the Baron said. Then he stepped out from behind the reception desk. 'Come and meet the others, Mr Armstrong.'

Baron Marackai led the man across the lobby and pushed open the double doors to an oak-panelled room. 'Can I offer you a drink?'

'Sure thing,' Mr Armstrong replied.

Blud shuffled over carrying a tray with two steaming cups of coffee.

Mr Armstrong took one and sipped it slowly, looking around the room.

Seated in leather armchairs around a roaring

log fire were three men and a woman. They were all wearing camouflage clothing and sipping hot coffee.

'Leave us now, Blud,' Baron Marackai said, taking a cup for himself. He stood beside the fireplace, facing the guests. 'And now for the introductions,' he said. 'Mr Armstrong, I'd like you to meet everyone. This is Herr Herman Pinkel.'

A man with a red face and a bulbous nose stood up and shook Mr Armstrong's hand. 'Sehr gut. Sehr gut,' Herr Herman Pinkel said.

The Baron gestured to a tall man with shiny hair tied in a ponytail. 'And this is Señor Pedro Pedroso.'

The man stood up and kissed Mr Armstrong on both cheeks. 'Encantado,' he said.

'And this is the delightful Lady Semolina,' the Baron continued.

A stern-looking woman with a curly moustache held out her hand.

Mr Armstrong took it and kissed it. 'Delighted,' he said. 'I think.'

'And this is Mr Zachariah D. Biggles.'

A big black man wearing dark sunglasses stood up. He towered over Mr Armstrong. 'You can call me Biggy.'

'Howdy y'all,' Mr Armstrong said. 'You can call me Chuck.'

'Take a seat please, Mr Armstrong,' Baron Marackai said.

Chuck Armstrong sat in a leather armchair and stretched his legs out in front of the fire.

'Firstly, let me welcome you all to Loadem Lodge,' Baron Marackai continued. 'It has always been my dream to reopen this marvellous hunting hideaway. As some of you may know, beast hunting is in my blood.'

'Bravo,' Lady Semolina said, twiddling her moustache.

'For too long beast hunts have been banned because some do-gooders think they are cruel,' the Baron told them.

'Down viz ze do-gooderz!' Herr Herman Pinkel said.

'But *I* say that hunting beasts is what humans are best at. It's as natural as starting fires and fighting wars. And this evening you lucky people will sample the thrills of the greatest beast-hunting range ever built – the Predatron!'

The guests clapped.

'Yee-ha!' Chuck Armstrong cheered.

Baron Marackai stepped over to a large table covered by a white sheet. 'Gentlemen, Lady Semolina, choose your fun!' he said.

He pulled back the sheet and the guests gasped. Underneath were five rifles with telescopic sights, a pair of pistols in leather holsters, a crossbow and longbow with quivers of arrows, a leather belt of knives, harpoon guns, hand grenades, a flame-thrower and boxes of titanium-tipped beast bullets.

'Olé!' Pedro Pedroso said.

'Tally-ho!' Lady Semolina said.

'When do we start?' Chuck Armstrong asked.

'All in good time,' Baron Marackai told him. 'We have smoked out the prey and it is being

prepared. We shall hunt it this evening.' He lifted his cup. 'TO THE THRILL OF THE KILL!'

The guests stood up, raising their cups to the Baron. 'The thrill of the kill!' they repeated.

The small man Blud shuffled in through the door and tugged on the Baron's fur coat.

'What is it, you horrible little twerp?' Baron Marackai asked.

'There's a helicopter coming, Sir,' Blud whispered. He led Baron Marackai to the window on the far side of the room and wiped the misted glass with his red rag. The Baron looked out into the snowy sky. In the distance was the outline of a white mountain. Above it a helicopter was coming in to land.

'Well, well, look who it is,' Baron Marackai said. 'Get the vehicles, Blud. You know what to do.'

CHAPTER EIGHT

Ulf's ears popped. The RSPCB helicopter was descending. 'We're landing,' he whispered to Tiana. He felt a jolt as Orson stepped from the flying cable, then heard a clanking sound as the giant unclipped the cable from the base of the helicopter. A few seconds later the helicopter touched down with a bump. Its engine stopped and Ulf heard the blades slowing.

'Stay quiet,' he whispered to Tiana.

From outside came muffled voices. Dr Fielding and Orson were talking. The door to the cargo hold slid open and Ulf felt a rush of cold air. He could hear the wind whistling outside. He hid under an old tarpaulin sheet as Orson reached in to unload the kit. Ulf heard the giant dragging his chainmail vest out of the helicopter.

'Could you pass me my rucksack, please?' Dr Fielding asked. 'And I'll need my caving boots.'

'What's the plan?' Orson asked.

'We'll have a look underground, check on the beasts and see if we can find this goblin.'

The door to the cargo hold slid shut. Ulf heard Orson and Dr Fielding getting kitted up, then they headed away from the helicopter.

'Let's go,' he whispered to Tiana. Ulf pushed off the tarpaulin sheet and gently opened the door. He squinted. Outside, a blizzard was blowing. Snowflakes were swirling and everything was bright white. They were on a snowy mountain that was dotted with caves. He saw Dr Fielding and Orson fifty metres away, heading to a cave with rocks around its entrance that looked like dragons' teeth. Dr Fielding was holding her GPRS tracker in her hand, and had her rucksack over her shoulder.

'Ready, Tiana?' Ulf asked.

Tiana wrapped herself in her red sycamore cloak with just her wings sticking out. 'It's chilly,' she said, flying through the gap in the door. She shivered, dodging the snowflakes.

As Dr Fielding and Orson entered the cave, Ulf jumped out of the cargo hold. His bare feet sunk into the snow.

'Won't you be cold?' Tiana asked.

'I'll be fine,' Ulf said. He was nearing his transformation. His blood was warming up and the hair on his hands and feet was starting to thicken. Tonight the moon would be full and he'd change from boy to wolf.

He looped the climbing rope over his shoulder, then headed across the snowy mountain towards the cave. He waited at the entrance, peering inside. At the back of the cave, a long dark tunnel sloped gradually downwards. He could see Orson and Dr Fielding heading along it. The giant was stooping, holding his lantern to light the way.

Ulf crept in, heading after them. 'Come on,

Tiana,' he whispered. Tiana flew beside him, glowing softly. They could hear the chittering sounds of underground beasts. Tiny eyes on stalks were peering from cracks in the walls.

'Friggs,' Ulf whispered. Frog-like beasts were watching them. Ulf trod carefully, feeling damp cold rock under his bare feet. Up ahead, Dr Fielding and Orson turned a corner, their lamplight slowly fading.

From the darkness, Ulf heard Dr Fielding calling, 'Gumball, are you here? It's the RSPCB-B-B.' Her voice echoed underground.

'The goblin's probably busy thieving,' Tiana said sharply.

'Ssh,' Ulf told her. 'If Dr Fielding finds out we're here, we'll be in big trouble.'

They crept round the corner at the end of the tunnel, but there was no sign of the light from Orson's lantern. Ulf switched on his head torch. He saw that the tunnel divided. Two passages led away in different directions.

'Which way did they go?' Tiana asked.

Ulf heard a noise from one of the passages. It

sounded like footsteps. 'Down here, Tiana,' he said, heading deeper into the mountain. The passage twisted and turned. As they crept along it, the sounds grew louder.

'Those aren't footsteps,' Tiana said.

Ulf listened. The sound was like daggers stabbing rock. He tiptoed into the darkness and the beam from his head torch shone down the passage, illuminating a large insect-like beast.

'Uh-oh,' Ulf said. Up ahead, stalking towards them along the tunnel, was a white beast with long articulated legs and two whip-like antennae. 'It's a cave mantis,' he whispered.

'Let's get out of here,' Tiana said.

'Just keep still. They're blind. It can't see us.'

The beast's eyelids were grown over. It was using its antennae to feel its way along the walls.

Ulf pressed his back against the side of the tunnel, and Tiana perched on his head torch.

'Stop fidgeting,' Ulf whispered.

'I'm not fidgeting.'

Ulf could hear something wriggling above him. A small lizard dropped down on to his

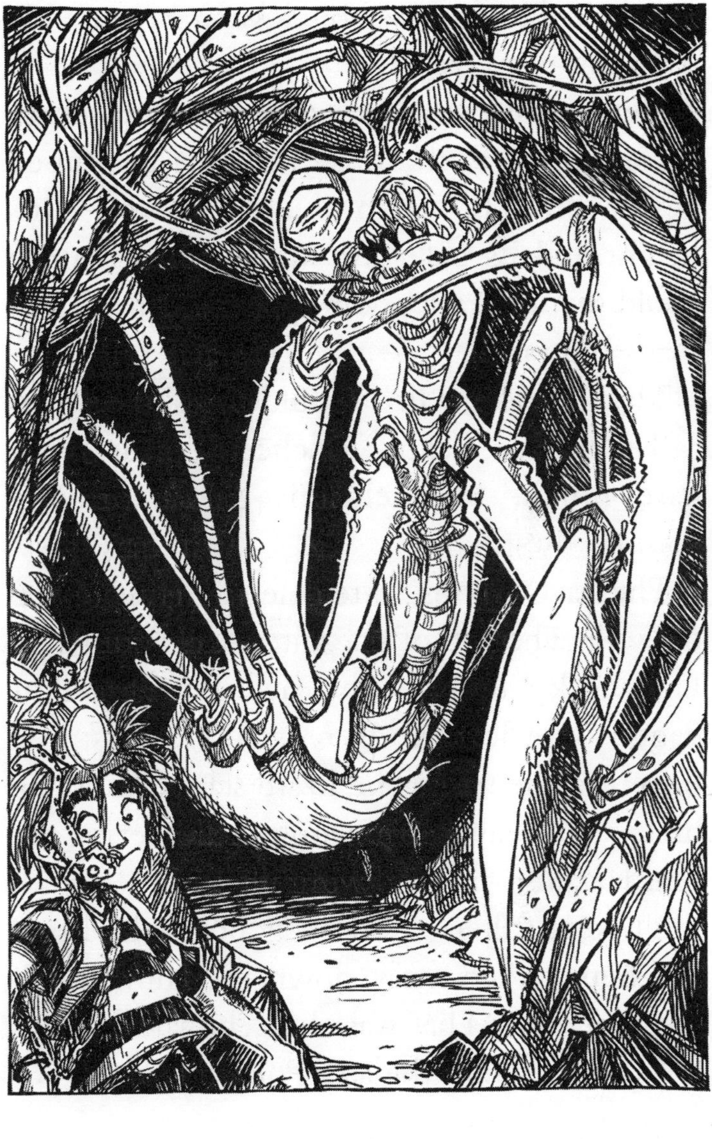

shoulder. He felt its foot tickling his ear. Ulf tried not to move.

He watched as the cave mantis approached, its antennae twitching. The beast stopped beside him. It was more than twice Ulf's height and its pale skin was so thin that he could see its heart beating and its belly full of toads and rats.

The lizard on Ulf's shoulder flicked out its forked tongue, licking his cheek, but he didn't dare flinch. He held his breath, staying completely still.

The cave mantis' antennae were feeling up the wall. The end of one antenna brushed over Ulf's neck. Suddenly, the cave mantis lifted its dagger-like leg, ready to strike. Ulf stayed frozen to the spot. The lizard started nibbling his ear. The cave mantis lunged, skewering the lizard against the rock.

Ulf kept still as the beast gobbled the lizard up then stalked away down the tunnel. Ulf breathed out. 'That was close,' he said.

Tiana flew into the air. 'Poor lizard.'

She flew down the tunnel, sparkling. 'Where did Dr Fielding and Orson go?'

'They've probably gone to look for the goblin,' Ulf said. He felt in his pocket and pulled out Professor Farraway's map. He unfolded it and, in the light from his head torch, traced his finger to the small cave labelled Gumball's Grotto.

'Well, which way is it?' Tiana asked.

Ulf looked carefully. 'I think we came in here,' he said, pointing to a jagged cavemouth. 'And the grotto's there.' He moved his finger. 'So that's down and west.'

He took the silver compass from his pocket, and checked which way the needle was pointing. 'West is this way,' he said, turning down a side tunnel.

He headed into a large underground chamber. Hanging from its ceiling were what looked like long spears of rock. There were hundreds of them, speckled in all different colours. They glistened in the light of Tiana's sparkles.

'They're beautiful,' Tiana said, weaving between them.

'Mind out, those are elephant leeches,' Ulf told her.

The spears of rock began rippling and swaying like the trunks of elephants, long leeches with fleshy suckers at their tips. They were reaching for Ulf and Tiana. One of them clamped on to Ulf's shoulder.

'No you don't,' Ulf said. He pulled the leech's sucker from his T-shirt, then he moved the leech aside and stepped past it. 'They're thirsty.'

Tiana weaved nervously among them as they coiled and turned towards her. 'I think they like my cloak,' she said.

'That's because it's red,' Ulf told her. 'The colour of blood.'

Tiana screamed and shot off through the chamber. Ulf pushed after her. 'They can suck more blood than a vampire,' he said. He was kicking through skin and bones on the ground.

At the far end of the chamber he stepped out into a tunnel.

He heard a faint echo: '—ball-all-all.'

'Listen, it's Dr Fielding,' Ulf whispered.

Her voice was coming from down the tunnel. 'Gumball, where are you-oo-oo?' Dr Fielding called.

Ulf and Tiana hurried towards the sound but the tunnel came to a dead end.

'Where is she?' Tiana asked.

'Gumball-all-all,' they heard again.

'It sounds like she's behind here,' Ulf said, pressing his ear to the wall at the end of the tunnel. The wall was warm and sticky, covered in a layer of mucus. He touched it with his hands. It was throbbing.

'That's not a wall. It's alive!' Tiana shrieked.

The wall was moving towards them. A hole opened in it, exposing a gummy mouth. It was a monstramaggot! It filled the width of the tunnel and was wriggling towards them.

'Eyugh!' Tiana said, darting back.

'Don't worry. It's perfectly harmless,' Ulf told her, wiping his slimy hand on his jeans. 'Monstramaggots only feed on bat poo.'

Tiana hovered in front of the enormous monstramaggot. 'It's revolting,' she said.

'We'll have to squeeze past it.'

'Yuck!' Tiana replied. She flew into the pocket of Ulf's jeans as he pressed himself against the side of the tunnel.

The monstramaggot began sliding past him, covering Ulf with slime. The slime soaked through Ulf's T-shirt and oozed down his jeans. The monstramaggot was a long one, six metres or more. Its sticky flesh rippled across his cheek, squishing him against the wall.

At last, with a slow sucking sound, the monstramaggot pushed past, and Ulf stepped back into the open tunnel behind it. His hair was clinging to his face. He shook his head and his hands, and slime flicked against the walls.

Tiana flew out of Ulf's pocket, shaking her delicate wings. They were dripping with monstramaggot mucus. She held her hand over her mouth, nearly vomiting. 'That was horrible,' she said.

Ulf wiped his head torch and looked down the tunnel. There was still no sign of Dr Fielding or Orson.

'Where did they go?' Tiana asked again.

'They must be nearby,' Ulf replied.

Tiana darted ahead, disappearing into an opening at the side of the tunnel. 'Look in here, Ulf,' she called.

Ulf ran to her, and saw the fairy hovering in a tall chamber.

'There are ropes in here,' she said. Tiana sparkled along a white rope that stretched across the chamber. 'Is this Gumball's Grotto?'

Ulf pulled out the Professor's map. By the light of his head torch, he found Leech Lair, then traced his finger along the tunnels.

'Ulf, look at this,' Tiana called.

Ulf looked over. The fairy was illuminating a dead owl wrapped in white rope. Ulf's head torch shone on another rope that ran vertically. He followed it up. It connected to another, then another. White silk ropes criss-crossed, stretching up to the ceiling. The dark cavern hid a huge white web, and hanging in it were dead owls, bats and shadowgulls.

Ulf looked again at the map. 'I don't think this is Gumball's Grotto,' he said nervously. 'This looks like Spider's Larder.'

Tiana squealed.

Ulf looked up. Descending from the ceiling on a rope of silk was an enormous wraith spider with hairy legs a metre long. It was glowing white with deadly venom. It dropped to the ground, hissing, and its jaws opened, exposing six mouths, each with razor-sharp fangs.

'Run!' Tiana screamed.

Ulf hurried through the chamber, clambering through the white ropes as Tiana flew ahead. They raced out the other side, then down a long tunnel. They could hear the spider scurrying after them.

Ulf ran as fast as he could.

'Hurry!' Tiana called.

Ahead, the beam from Ulf's head torch lit a large opening in the side of the tunnel. 'In there, Tiana! Hide!' Ulf called.

'Turn off your light!' Tiana said.

Ulf switched off his light and Tiana extinguished her sparkles so the spider couldn't see them. They dived through the large opening. It was pitch dark inside.

'Tiana?' Ulf whispered.

'I'm right here,' she said.

Ulf felt her wings fluttering against his cheek. He crouched low, hearing the spider coming up the tunnel. He could just make out its glowing white shape as it scurried past.

'Phew,' Tiana said.

As Tiana spoke, Ulf heard the spider stop.

For a moment there was silence.

Tap-tap-tap-tap. Tap-tap-tap-tap. The spider was coming back along the tunnel.

Ulf saw a hairy leg step through the opening. 'Oh dear,' he whispered.

The spider hissed. Then Ulf heard a loud grunting sound behind him and the spider quickly retreated. It scurried back down the tunnel.

'We're safe,' Tiana said.

'What was that noise?' Ulf whispered.

From behind them, in the dark, came another grunt then a low snuffling.

'It smells in here,' Tiana said.

Ulf sniffed. It did smell, of old meat and beast dung. He switched on his head torch and Tiana turned on her sparkles.

They were crouched in a vast underground chamber, bigger than a barn and twice as high. **All around them, staring from the shadows, were huge green trolls.**

CHAPTER NINE

'Run!' Tiana said.

Ulf jumped to his feet, but the exit was blocked by an enormous male troll. More trolls were gathering on all sides. 'We're trapped, Tiana,' he said.

They were surrounded by over twenty trolls, the biggest Ulf had ever seen, with hairy chins and long tusks that grew from their lower lips.

'They look hungry,' Tiana said.

The trolls were edging nearer, drooling and slobbering, dragging their knuckles along the ground.

Some began growling. Others stood upright beating their chests. 'Oof! Oof! Oof!'

All around Ulf and Tiana, the trolls were closing in. One lunged at Tiana, swiping with its huge clawed hand. Tiana darted back.

Ulf heard a growl behind him. He swung round and saw a troll lumbering towards him, its huge tusks ready to strike. His head torch shone in its face and the troll stopped, holding its arm up to shield its eyes.

'They don't like the light,' Ulf said. He swung his head torch from one troll to the next. Tiana started flying in circles around him, glowing brightly, trying to keep the trolls away. But as each troll stepped back, another edged forward. 'Oof! Oof! Oof! Oof!'

Saliva was dribbling down their chins.

'Help!' Tiana screamed. 'They're going to eat us!'

Just then, Ulf heard loud thumping footsteps. He looked across to one of the tunnels coming off the chamber and saw lantern light.

It was Orson! The giant was running towards them.

'Orson! In here!' Ulf called.

Orson the giant burst into the Troll Chamber, his lantern held in front of him.

The trolls turned and growled.

'Help!' Tiana cried, flying up.

'Over here!' Ulf called from behind the trolls.

'Ulf! Tiana! Is that you?' Orson asked, peering over the trolls' heads. 'What are you doing here?'

One of the trolls charged at the giant. Its tusks clattered against Orson's chainmail vest. The giant stood firm and the troll charged again. Orson gripped one of its tusks, pushing the troll backwards.

The troll was fierce and strong, but it was no match for Orson.

The giant let the troll go, then turned up the gas on his lantern. The light grew brighter and all the trolls started backing away. 'They're beauties, aren't they, Ulf?' Orson said, striding further inside, swinging the lantern. 'That's it. Back you go,' he told the trolls.

Ulf watched as the trolls retreated to the edges of the chamber.

'You don't want to get caught by hungry longtusks,' Orson told him.

Ulf heard more footsteps as Dr Fielding came running down the tunnel shining a torch. She stopped at the entrance to the chamber. 'Ulf? Tiana?' she said. She marched in.

'You're in trouble now,' Orson whispered. He was swinging his lantern to keep the trolls back.

'What on earth are you two doing here?' Dr Fielding asked.

'It's my fault, Dr Fielding,' Ulf said. 'I wanted to come on the expedition.'

'But how did you get here?'

'In the back of the helicopter.'

Dr Fielding stared at Ulf in disbelief. 'It's not safe for you here.'

She shone her torch around the trolls. They were still grunting and growling.

'Sorry, Dr Fielding,' Ulf said, hanging his head.

Dr Fielding turned to the little fairy. 'And you should know better, Tiana.'

Tiana glowed with embarrassment. 'Sorry, Dr Fielding.'

Ulf stared at the ground. It was black. He bent down and wiped his hand over the chamber floor. It was covered in black dust. 'Look, Dr Fielding,' he said, showing her his hand.

Dr Fielding rubbed it. 'That's soot,' she said. She looked around the chamber. In the light of Orson's lantern, the walls looked black too. 'What's happened in here?' she asked.

She looked more closely at the trolls, taking care not to shine her torch in their eyes. Some of them had blackened skin. An adult female was scraping its sooty stomach. A wrinkled old troll with broken tusks was chewing a sooty bone. A male was grooming a female, trying to clean black soot from her back.

'Why are they sooty?' Ulf whispered.

Dr Fielding started walking very slowly towards the trolls. 'I don't know. It's odd.'

Orson held his lantern up to protect her. Ulf and Tiana followed.

As the trolls edged away from the light, Ulf noticed a big male lying on its side on the ground. A female was bent over the troll, licking its skin.

'That big one doesn't look well,' Tiana said, hovering close to Ulf.

Ulf took a step towards it.

The female troll turned and growled.

'Be careful,' Orson said. He swung his lantern from side to side and the female troll slowly backed away. 'That's it, girl. Give us a little space.'

Dr Fielding stepped to the big male troll lying on the ground. 'Stand guard please, Orson. I need to inspect it.'

While the giant stood over the troll with his lantern raised, Dr Fielding knelt down beside it. The troll wasn't moving.

Ulf watched. 'Is it alive?' he asked.

Tiana perched on the troll's shoulder. 'It's still warm.'

'Help me roll it over, Ulf,' Dr Fielding said.

Ulf and Dr Fielding gripped the troll's tusks and heaved, rolling it on to its back.

Dr Fielding pressed her ear to the troll's mouth and listened. 'It's only just breathing,' she said. She lifted the troll's wrinkled eyelids. Its eyes were cloudy. 'It's barely conscious.'

The troll coughed, and sticky black phlegm splattered its hairy chin.

Dr Fielding took off her rucksack and pulled out a packet of cotton wool. She wiped the black phlegm from its lips. With both hands she prised open the troll's mouth, then shone her torch inside.

'Urgh,' Tiana said, smelling the troll's breath. Ulf sniffed. It stank.

He stared at the troll's teeth. They were crooked and chipped, with bits of meat and fur stuck between them. Its tongue was thick and pitted. Its whole mouth was black with soot.

'It looks as if it has inhaled smoke,' Dr Fielding said.

'Smoke?' Ulf asked.

'See how swollen its throat is.'

Ulf looked to the back of the troll's mouth. The opening to its windpipe was constricted and its breathing sounded strained.

The troll snorted and more black phlegm leaked from its nose.

Dr Fielding handed the cotton wool to Ulf. 'Clean that up while I check its lungs,' she said.

Ulf started wiping the troll's nose. He put his finger up its nostrils, trying to clear its airways. The hairs inside the troll's nose felt bristly as he scooped out lumps of black gunk.

Dr Fielding held her stethoscope to the troll's chest and listened. 'Its lungs sound blocked,' she said.

The troll coughed. Then, as it tried to breathe in, it choked.

'What's happening?' Ulf asked.

The troll wheezed, then stopped breathing altogether.

'It's in respiratory arrest!' Dr Fielding said.

The troll lay still, as if it were dead.

Dr Fielding felt its wrist, checking for a pulse. 'Its heart's stopped. Stand back, Ulf.'

Ulf stepped back and watched as Dr Fielding placed both hands on the centre of the troll's broad green chest. She interlocked her fingers and, with her arms straight, started pressing down hard, again and again.

'What are you doing?' Ulf asked.

'Cardiopulmonary resuscitation,' Dr Fielding explained. 'CPR. We've got to get its heart and lungs working.'

She quickly placed her hand under the troll's hairy chin and tilted its head back to open its windpipe. Then she covered the troll's nose with both hands and took a deep breath.

Ulf watched as Dr Fielding opened her mouth and leant forwards, pressing her mouth over the troll's rubbery lips.

'Eyugh!' Tiana said, looking away. 'She's kissing the troll!'

Dr Fielding steadily breathed out into the troll's mouth.

'She's trying to help it breathe,' Ulf said.

Dr Fielding sat up and pushed the troll's chest again. It still wasn't moving. She took another breath and placed her mouth over the troll's, breathing air into it.

'Come on, troll. You can do it,' Ulf said.

Dr Fielding blew once more into the troll's mouth.

Suddenly, the troll coughed and its body convulsed.

Dr Fielding pulled her head away, wiping her lips.

The troll coughed again, splattering thick black phlegm over its tusks. It shook its head. It was breathing!

Dr Fielding took a bottle and a syringe from her rucksack. She quickly gave the troll an injection of adrenaline.

The troll grunted and licked its tusks, then rolled on to all fours.

'Move back, everyone,' Dr Fielding said.

Huddled under Orson's lantern, they all stepped away from the injured troll. As they did so, the female troll lumbered back over.

The two beasts touched tusks and snorted.

'What do you think happened to it?' Ulf asked.

Dr Fielding looked around. 'There's been a fire down here,' she said.

'A fire? Underground?'

Orson leant down, frowning in the lamplight. 'Fires don't just start by themselves.'

* * *

As the snow fell on Honeycomb Mountain, a cattle truck and an oil tanker wound their way up the icy track. They stopped near the top where the track finished.

The door of the oil tanker opened and Bone climbed down into the snow. From the side of the oil tanker he began unreeling a long hose.

Blud jumped out of the cattle truck with his rifle slung over his back. He glanced towards the RSPCB helicopter parked on the mountain. 'Deal with that, Bone,' he said.

The big man trudged to the helicopter and bent its blades with a metal hook.

Blud clambered to the oily hole at the top of the mountain. 'The RSPCB are doomed,' he sniggered, wiping his runny nose with a snotty red rag.

Bone dragged the hose from the oil tanker and headed after him. 'I always have to do the heavy work,' the big man grumbled.

Blud took the rifle from his shoulder. 'You're the oil man, I'm the shooter. If you've got a problem with that, talk to the Baron.'

Bone shoved the hose down the hole. He turned the nozzle on. There was a gurgling sound as thick black oil gushed from its end, pumping into the mountain.

Blud took a box of matches from his pocket. 'Time to warm them up.'

CHAPTER TEN

Dr Fielding shone her torch around the trolls. 'No other serious injuries,' she said.

Ulf was beside her. He felt a drip on his head and looked up. Another drip fell, then another. All around, drips began splashing on to the floor of the Troll Chamber. It was as if it was beginning to rain deep inside the mountain. He wiped his hair. Black liquid clung to his fingers. 'What's happening?' he asked.

Dr Fielding shone her torch on the roof of the chamber. 'It looks like oil,' she said.

Ulf could hear it trickling down the walls.

'Where's it coming from?' Orson asked.

Trolls started beating their chests. 'Oof! Oof! Oof! Oof!'

Some banged the walls with their fists.

As more oil poured down from the roof of the chamber, Tiana darted into Ulf's pocket to protect herself.

Suddenly, there was a roaring sound as the oil caught fire. Flames swirled around the ceiling and spread down the walls.

'Take cover!' Orson yelled. He threw his arms around Dr Fielding and Ulf, shielding them as flaming oil splashed to the ground.

The trolls charged for the exits.

The chamber was filling with smoke – thick, black smoke that made Ulf's eyes sting and bit into the back of his throat. He pulled his T-shirt up over his mouth.

'Get out!' Orson shouted. 'I'll get the trolls.'

Ulf tried to run, but in the thick smoke he could hardly see. He was coughing and choking. Flames were roaring around him. Trolls were crashing past him, barging him to the side as they raced to escape.

'Ulf! Over here,' he heard.

Ulf caught a glimpse of Dr Fielding's torch and staggered towards it. But at that moment, a sheet of flames fell in front of him. He shielded his face from the fire. 'It's no use!' he called. He was being pushed back by the heat.

A troll thumped into him and Ulf was knocked to the ground.

'Get up, Ulf,' Tiana called from his pocket.

He scrambled to his feet and staggered to the back of the burning chamber, following a group of stampeding trolls into a narrow exit. He'd lost Orson and Dr Fielding.

'We've got to get outside,' Tiana called. 'Run!'

Ulf ran as fast as he could up a back tunnel, slipping and sliding over the rocks. He heard a blast and glanced back as the chamber erupted in a fireball behind him.

The fireball hurled him through the air, and he landed with a thump, his head crashing against the tunnel wall. The lamp on his head torch smashed.

'Ulf, are you okay?' he heard from his pocket.

But everything was a blur. The bang to Ulf's head had injured him. He felt dizzy.

Then he felt his ankle being gripped by a bony hand. He was being dragged along the floor of the tunnel, and pulled into a cool dark cave. He heard a boulder being rolled across the entrance, cutting off the smoke.

Ulf felt himself losing consciousness. Tiana flew from his pocket, and in her glow he could just make out the face of a beast with white eyes, pointy ears and a fat snout.

A goblin was leaning over him.

'Gumball!' Ulf managed to say. Then everything went black.

CHAPTER ELEVEN

Ulf opened his eyes. He was lying on his back, staring up at the roof of a cave. He sniffed. The cave smelt musty. He felt his head. There was a big bump on his scalp.

'Give that back!' he heard.

Ulf sat up and coughed. His mouth tasted of smoke. At the back of the cave, he saw Tiana's light. She was buzzing angrily above Gumball. The goblin was in the shadows, his bony hands clutching Ulf's broken head torch.

'Mine now,' the goblin said. 'My shiny.'

'It's not yours,' Tiana said indignantly. She pulled the strap of the head torch as hard as she could. 'It's Ulf's.'

‘Tiana, what’s going on?’ Ulf asked.

Tiana glanced over at him. ‘Ulf, you’re awake! You’ve been out for hours,’ she told him.

At that moment, the goblin yanked the strap of the head torch from Tiana’s grip. ‘Bad luck, fairy,’ he told her. ‘My shiny now.’

Ulf looked around. He was in Gumball’s Grotto. By the light of Tiana’s sparkles, he could see shiny metal objects dotting the walls: tin cans, bottle tops and coins.

‘Let him have it, Tiana. It’s broken anyway,’ Ulf said.

‘But he’s a thief,’ Tiana replied.

‘He saved our lives,’ Ulf told her.

‘He only wanted your head torch.’

The goblin hugged the head torch and started polishing it against his chest. ‘My shiny shiny,’ he muttered.

‘You’re a selfish beast,’ Tiana said to him.

The goblin looked across at Ulf and grinned. His teeth were black and broken, his face was dirty, and wispy grey hairs sprouted from his wrinkled skin.

'We've been looking for you, Gumball,' Ulf said. 'We got your message.'

'What message?' Gumball asked.

'Your messenger bat. It arrived yesterday.'

The little goblin smiled. 'My bat's safe?'

'It's at the RSPCB.'

The goblin stopped smiling and started trembling. 'I didn't send the messenger bat,' he said. Gumball stepped back into the shadows, clutching the head torch. '*He* did.'

'*He?*' Ulf asked, puzzled.

Gumball placed the head torch on a ledge on the wall, then started rearranging his shiny objects.

Tiana flew over and kicked a shiny tin can to the floor. 'Goblin, what are you talking about?'

The little goblin picked the can up and started polishing it.

'Who sent the messenger bat, Gumball?' Ulf asked.

The goblin's hand was shaking as he polished. 'Nasty man,' he said. 'Nasty man took my bat.'

'What nasty man?' Tiana asked.

The goblin raised his shaky hand and turned down his little finger. 'Nasty man missing finger.'

Ulf and Tiana gasped.

'Marackai!' Ulf said.

'Marackai's *here*?' Tiana shrieked.

'When did you see this man, Gumball?' Ulf asked.

'A day ago. Out there.' Gumball pointed to the ceiling.

Ulf looked up and saw a hole. He stepped to the wall and climbed up, poking his head into the hole. He felt cold air on his face. 'Come on, Tiana.'

Ulf squeezed through the hole and began pulling himself up a long craggy shaft, gripping hold of its rocky sides.

'Where are you going, Ulf?' Tiana called, flying after him.

'We have to warn Dr Fielding,' he called to her. He climbed higher and higher until he saw a layer of snow above him. He pushed up through the snow into bright daylight. Ulf squinted, wiping the snow from his head. He was at the top of Honeycomb Mountain. The blizzard had stopped and the sky was clearing.

Ulf climbed out and saw trolls lying on the ground. Tiana flew out behind him.

'What's happened?' she asked.

Ulf rushed to a troll and found a feathered dart stuck into its arm. It was snoring. 'They've been tranquillized,' he said, puzzled.

Ulf saw bootprints in the snow where humans had been walking. He traced them to a hole that was black and oily. On the ground was a matchbox. He picked it up. 'That fire was started on purpose!' he said.

Just then, Gumball the goblin poked his head out from his hole. 'Nasty man smoked out the trolls,' the little goblin said. 'He took the young ones away.'

'Ulf, look!' Tiana called. She was hovering over a rucksack that was half buried in the snow. It was Dr Fielding's. Orson's lantern lay smashed a short distance away. Ulf ran over and saw a crater in the snow the size of the giant and a long trench running to an icy track as if Orson had been dragged away. Ulf could see tyre marks on the track that led down the mountain. He looked across at the RSPCB helicopter. Its blades had been bent.

'Tiana, it was a trap!' he said. 'Marackai sent that message. And now he's taken Dr Fielding and Orson!'

'Taken them?' Tiana asked. 'Where?'

Ulf turned to the little goblin. 'Gumball, did you see where the nasty man went?' he asked.

'Bad place,' Gumball muttered.

'Gumball, we need to know,' Ulf said.

Gumball scurried over and tapped the matchbox in Ulf's hand. Ulf looked at it. On the matchbox was a picture of a wooden building. 'Loadem Lodge,' he read.

The goblin scuttled to the edge of the mountain.

'Where are you going?' Ulf called, running after him. Ulf stopped suddenly. It was a sheer drop down.

Gumball pointed north to the far end of a long valley. In the distance, Ulf could just make out a wooden building at the base of a hill. A thin trail of smoke was rising from its chimney…

* * *

In the hunter's lounge of Loadem Lodge, Baron Marackai was standing at the fireplace, a log fire crackling behind him as he finished telling a story. 'And that's how I bagged my first troll,' he said, smiling.

The guests cheered.

'Awesome!' Chuck Armstrong said.

'Tell us another one,' Lady Semolina said.

Baron Marackai fetched a large leatherbound photograph album from a cabinet at the side of the room. 'You'll enjoy this,' he said, laying it on a coffee table in front of his guests.

The guests turned the pages of the photograph album one at a time, their eyes wide with excitement.

'Those were the days,' Baron Maracakai said. 'Oh, to have lived then!'

The album was full of old black-and-white photographs of beast hunters, each proudly holding up the head of a dead beast mounted on a plaque.

'Now *zat* iz vot I call hunting,' Herr Herman Pinkel said.

'Those guys were real experts,' Chuck Armstrong added.

'Great men, all of them,' the Baron said. '*Real* men.'

He gave Lady Semolina a wink. She giggled and licked her moustache.

Then the door opened. The Baron looked round as Blud stepped in. 'What is it, Blud? Can't you see I'm enthralling these people with my stories?'

'It's all done, Sir,' Blud told him.

'Splendid,' the Baron replied, ushering the small man back out into the lobby. He closed the door behind him. 'Were they all there?' he asked.

'No, Sir,' Blud replied. 'Just the vet and the giant.'

'Are you certain?'

'Yes, Sir.'

'Oh, what a shame,' the Baron sighed. 'I had hoped the werewolf would come too. It's a full moon tonight. I wanted his beast head for my wall.'

Blud sneezed, then wiped his nose with his snotty red rag. 'What shall we do with the prisoners? Can we kill them now?'

'Not yet,' the Baron told him. 'I have plans for them. We're going to have a little fun tonight!'

CHAPTER TWELVE

'Come on, Ulf. We have to get to Loadem Lodge,' Tiana called, flying towards the long winding track that led down the mountain.

Ulf unfolded Professor Farraway's map. 'Wait a second,' he told her. On the map was a long hollow shaft that spiralled down through the centre of the mountain. The Corkscrew, he read. 'There's a quicker way.'

Ulf took the silver compass from his pocket to check his bearings.

The little goblin reached out and touched the compass. 'Shiny,' he said.

Tiana came flying back. 'You're not having that, Gumball,' she said.

‘Sorry, Gumball, I need this,’ Ulf told him, checking which way the compass needle was pointing. He looked at the little goblin. Gumball’s eyes were fixed on the shiny silver.

‘Thanks for your help,’ Ulf said. ‘But I’m afraid we have to go now.’

Ulf turned and ran off through the snow, looking for a square-sided cave. ‘In here, Tiana,’ he called.

Tiana flew over and darted after Ulf into the cave. Her sparkles illuminated the walls.

Ulf navigated using the Professor’s map. He squeezed along narrow passageways and ducked through openings. Every so often he heard the sound of little footsteps behind him.

Gumball was following.

‘What’s he doing?’ Ulf asked.

‘He wants your compass,’ Tiana said.

‘Maybe he just wants to help,’ Ulf told her.

Ulf stopped and glanced back up the tunnel. The goblin scurried behind a rock.

‘Gumball!’ Ulf called. ‘It’s okay. You can come with us.’

Gumball was hiding.

'Goblins are so shifty,' Tiana said. 'Come on, leave him.'

Ulf turned and continued down the tunnel. He led the way to a round chamber with damp walls. In its centre was a large hole in the floor. Water was trickling into it.

'Are you sure this is the way?' Tiana asked.

'It says so on the Professor's map,' Ulf replied. He peered down the hole. It fell away into blackness. He picked up a stone and dropped it down. He heard it clattering against rock, counting to twenty as the sounds became fainter. 'This must be the Corkscrew.'

'It sounds a long way down,' Tiana said. 'Are you sure it's safe?'

'We have to hurry,' Ulf replied. He slipped the map and compass into his pockets, then sat on the edge of the hole. 'See you at the bottom.'

Ulf dropped feet-first into the hole and shot downwards, sliding against the wet walls of a narrow shaft. Water sprayed into his eyes and mouth and a *whooshing* sound roared in his ears as he gathered speed. The shaft was pitch black. It twisted and turned round and round like a corkscrew. He was hurtling faster and faster down through the mountain.

Suddenly, he felt the walls vanish. He was falling through air. Below, he could hear the roar of rushing water. He landed with a splash, plunging into an ice-cold underground river. Ulf sank, tumbling and twisting. He kicked his legs and swam to the surface.

'Are you okay?' he heard. He looked up and saw Tiana zooming down towards him, her sparkles illuminating the water. Ulf gasped. He was being swept away. He saw his map being washed downriver, and his rope uncoiling from his shoulder in the current. Ulf grabbed its end.

'Over here, Ulf,' Tiana called, flying to a rocky shore at the edge of the river. Ulf kicked frantically, swimming as hard as he could, fighting against the current. He reached for the rocks, grabbing hold of them, then pulled himself out. Behind him, he heard a splash.

'What was that?' he asked.

Tiana flew out across the water. By her light, Ulf saw pointy ears surface in the river.

'Oh no, it's Gumball,' Tiana cried.

The little goblin was struggling to stay afloat, his arms thrashing. 'Help!' he called. He was being dragged along by the current.

Downriver, Ulf saw a line of yellow fins rise from the water. He watched in horror as the huge head of a sword serpent broke the surface. 'Gumball, swim!' he called.

Tiana was flying above the little goblin. 'Gumball, swim, you idiot!' she yelled. 'You'll get eaten!'

The goblin was being washed towards the serpent.

'Gumball, watch out!' Ulf called.

The serpent opened its jaws, its fangs glinting like swords.

Quickly, Ulf tied a loop in his rope to make a lasso. He swung the lasso over his head, then threw it. The serpent lunged. The lasso looped around Gumball, and Ulf tugged. The serpent's jaws slammed shut, just missing the goblin. Ulf pulled on the rope as fast as he could, dragging Gumball through the water. The sword serpent thrashed its tail and followed. It hissed as Ulf heaved Gumball on to the rocks, then it butted the shore and disappeared back under the water. The soaking-wet goblin lay on the rocks, spluttering.

'Are you okay, Gumball?' Ulf asked.

'You silly beast,' Tiana said, darting over. 'You could have died.'

Gumball squirted water from his mouth. 'Gumball coming too,' he said.

Ulf smiled, then pulled out his compass, trying to work out which way to go next.

Gumball reached out his bony hand. 'Gimme,' he said to Ulf.

Tiana slapped the goblin's finger. 'You ungrateful beast,' she said. 'Is that stupid compass all you can think about? Ulf just saved your life.'

Gumball drew his hand back slowly.

'Come on,' Ulf said, slipping the compass safely back into his pocket. 'It's not far now.'

CHAPTER THIRTEEN

Blud and Bone were at work in the dungeons below Loadem Lodge.

The big man Bone walked along a row of cages, throwing buckets of water through the bars.

In each cage a troll woke up and growled.

Blud reached into a wooden crate and pulled out a meaty steak. 'Dinner time,' he said, dangling it in front of the cages.

The trolls lumbered forwards, clattering their tusks against the metal bars. They grunted, reaching for the meat.

'They're hungry,' Bone said, grinning.

The trolls were drooling.

Blud wafted the meaty steak in front of them. 'Lovely juicy meat!' he said.

The trolls rammed the bars of the cages, snorting and slobbering.

'But you're not having it.'

Blud pulled the meat away and Bone laughed.

'They're starving,' Bone said.

'That's how the Baron wants them,' Blud told him.

From his jacket pocket Blud took out a large sewing needle and a ball of string. He grabbed lots more meaty steaks from the crate, then sat on the floor, stitching them all together.

'What are you doing?' Bone asked.

'You'll see,' Blud replied.

While Blud stitched, the trolls rattled the bars with their tusks. They were watching him, groaning with hunger.

Bone picked out the biggest, juiciest steak he could find. 'Can I eat one?' he asked.

'No!' Blud said. 'Give that here.'

When Blud had stitched together all the steaks from the crate, he held up a big blanket of meat.

'What's that for?' Bone asked.

'It's part of the Baron's plan,' Blud told him.

Blud carried the blanket of meat out of the dungeons, heading through a stone archway and along a corridor. Flaming torches lined the walls, lighting doors on either side. Bone watched as Blud carried the blanket of meat through a door marked BAIT ROOM. A moment later he came back out, grinning. He wiped his hands on his trousers.

'What have you done with it?' Bone asked.

'It's a surprise,' Blud said, tapping the side of his nose. 'You'll have to wait and see.' The small man stepped across the corridor to a door marked TROPHY PROCESSING ROOM. 'Come on. It's time to grease the guillotine.'

Both men stepped inside. In the centre of the room stood a tall contraption. This was the guillotine, a machine used to remove the heads of hunted beasts as trophies. It looked like a large metal bench with chains across it, and two steel uprights at one end. Between the uprights was a big metal blade.

Rats scurried across the room, sniffing around a basket on the floor at the end of the guillotine.

Blud kicked his way through the rats and jumped up on to the bench. 'Get the grease,' he said.

From a tub in the corner of the room, Bone scooped out a handful of grease. He rubbed the grease up and down the steel uprights.

'Let's try it,' Blud said. The small man took a meaty steak from his pocket and handed it to Bone. 'Stick this under the blade.' He pulled on a rope at the side of the guillotine and the big metal blade started lifting up.

Bone laid the meat on the end of the bench.

Rats started jumping up, trying to nibble it.

Blud was singing: '**You are the greaser. Grease, grease, grease. I am the chopper. Chop, chop, chop.**' He let go of the rope and the metal blade dropped between the uprights.

It thudded down, chopping the meat in two. A bloody chunk of steak fell into the basket on the floor. Rats scurried over, climbing into the basket to gobble the meat up.

'Blud! Bone!' they heard. 'Where are you?'

Footsteps were coming along the corridor outside. The door opened and Baron Marackai looked in. He saw the meat in the basket. 'You're not to play with the guillotine!' he shouted. 'We'll need that nice and sharp for after the hunt. We'll be making trophies from the trolls' heads.'

Blud jumped down from the bench. 'Sorry, Baron,' he said.

A rat scampered up Blud's trouser leg.

'Are the giant and the vet secure?' the Baron asked.

'Yes, Baron,' Blud said, hopping and wriggling. He shook his leg.

'Then it's time to prepare the Predatron. I want all the machines checked.'

Blud squealed as the rat nibbled.

'And stop messing around!'

CHAPTER FOURTEEN

With the sound of the river fading behind them, Ulf and Tiana crept down a narrow passageway. They came to a dead end.

'We're lost,' Tiana said.

Ulf took out his compass, checking his bearings.

Gumball crept beside him. 'Gumball help,' the goblin said.

Gumball reached out and tapped his bony knuckles against the wall. It sounded as if the wall was made of metal.

Ulf pushed against it and a sheet of rusty corrugated iron bent outwards. 'Thanks Gumball,' he said, ducking through.

He came out in a wide tunnel that was lit by a line of electric light bulbs.

Tiana flew after him. 'What is this place?' she asked.

The line of bulbs stretched in either direction, and railtracks ran along the ground. The tunnel was made of rusting iron. Ladders were bolted to the walls, leading up and down through hatches.

Gumball scurried to Ulf's side. 'Nasty here,' he muttered.

'What do you mean, Gumball?' Ulf asked.

'Professor shut it long time ago.'

'Professor Farraway?'

Gumball stepped into the light. 'Professor friend. Professor made me spotter,' he said proudly.

'I can't think why,' Tiana muttered. She flew off down the tunnel.

The little goblin looked at Ulf, grinning with his broken teeth. 'Gumball good spotter. I see everything.'

Ulf saw Gumball's eyes creeping towards his compass. He slipped it back in his pocket.

'Ulf, look at this,' Tiana called.

Ulf ran to look. The fairy was hovering by a contraption on a wrought-iron stand. It looked like a huge metal box with a large tube poking from it. It had a mechanism of springs, rubber belts and freshly-greased cogs. Inside the box, Ulf could see big black balls, and on its side was a lever. A sign read **STICKY STUCKY**.

'What is this, Gumball?' Ulf asked. He turned back. The goblin was creeping up behind him, reaching for his pocket.

Gumball quickly pulled his hand back and started biting his dirty fingernails. 'Hunters built the machines,' he mumbled. He pointed to a hatch in the wall that was bolted shut. 'They hunted beasts out there.'

Ulf slid the bolt sideways and swung the hatch open. Daylight flooded in as he looked across a wide snowy valley. In its middle, a tall metal pole was sticking out of the ground. Hanging from the top of the pole, on a chain, was a large metal ball.

Further down the valley, he could make out

the long metal arm of a crane. It was white with fresh snow, and on its end was a big mechanical claw.

On the ground by the crane, he saw the snow move. A hatch lifted open and a big man with a thick beard climbed out, carrying a pot and a shovel. Behind him came a small man dabbing his nose with a red rag.

'Look,' Ulf said.

It was the Baron's men.

'What are they doing?' Tiana asked, flying to Ulf's shoulder.

The big man began shovelling snow from the base of the crane. As he dug, Ulf heard a clang. It sounded like the ground beneath the snow was made of metal too.

Nearby, the small man poked the snow with a stick, and a large metal disc sprang up on a spring. 'Bone, here's one!' he called.

The big man trudged over carrying the pot. He dipped his hand in, scooping out a lump of grease. He greased the spring, then pushed the disc back under the snow.

Ulf looked along the valley. He saw metal pipes poking up from the snow. On the sides of the valley he could make out snowy balconies and spotlights. The valley was entirely man-made. 'I don't like the look of this, Tiana,' he said, closing the hatch. 'We should hurry.'

Ulf set off along the tunnel with Tiana flying after him. Beside the railtrack he found a four-wheeled cart turned upside down. Ulf turned the cart over.

'What are you doing, Ulf?' Tiana asked.

The cart had a wooden seat and pedals on the floor. Ulf lifted it on to the tracks and sat in it. 'We'll go faster in this,' he said.

He started pedalling and the cart began to move. Tiana perched on the front, holding on tightly as they picked up speed.

Gumball came running after them.

'Oh no, are you coming too, Gumball?' Tiana asked.

The goblin caught up and hopped in behind Ulf. 'Gumball be passenger,' he said.

As they rolled forwards, the tunnel widened. Above them, Ulf saw huge iron pistons stretching from one wall to the other. He pedalled past a sign saying **THE CRUSHER**.

The track weaved between girders, cables and pipes. It was as if they were inside the workings of a huge machine. Ulf pedalled harder. Up ahead the track divided. One route continued straight; the other looped left and downwards. The cart veered to the left.

Tiana shrieked as they whirled down.

Ulf lifted his feet. The pedals were spinning. 'This is more like it!' he called.

Tiana clung to the front of the cart, trying not to be blown away.

'We're going under the valley,' Ulf said.

The track twisted and turned and the cart sped down between dozens of metal columns. The columns rose from floor to ceiling. Ulf saw more tracks running off into the darkness as they shot past a sign saying **FOREST OF FEAR**. Above him, through metal grilles, Ulf could see snow.

The track weaved, then twisted upwards again. Ulf pedalled up a slope and the wheels squeaked. As he reached the top, the cart lurched round a bend and Ulf saw a sign saying **DROWNING POOL**.

Gumball stood up and leaned forwards. 'Wolfy pedal good,' he said.

'Sit down,' Ulf said. 'You'll fall out.'

Gumball wobbled and fell on to Ulf. 'Oopsy,' the goblin said, grinning. He sat back down as the track straightened.

They passed shelves full of boulders lined up above a metal chute. The chute was poking out into the valley. **SKITTLE ALLEY**, another sign read.

'Look, Ulf!' Tiana said, pointing ahead.

The track was coming to an end. Ulf saw empty pedal-carts parked in a circle. Beyond them was a big wooden door.

Gumball pulled a lever on the side of the cart and it squeaked to a halt. He hopped out and scuttled behind the pedal-carts. 'Loadem Lodge behind that door,' he said. 'Good luck.'

He was holding something in his hands.

'Hang on, what's that you've got?' Tiana asked suspiciously. She flew over to Gumball.

The little goblin was clutching Ulf's compass.

'Hey! Give that back, slimeball!' Tiana cried.

'Mine now,' Gumball said. 'My shiny.'

'Thief!' Tiana said. 'Ulf, he picked your pocket!'

Gumball clutched the compass to his chest.

Ulf climbed out of the pedal-cart. 'It's okay, Gumball, you can keep it now,' he told him.

'Keep?' Gumball asked.

'Yes,' Ulf replied.

Gumball stepped forwards. He was smiling. 'Friend,' he said, holding out his bony hand.

Ulf shook it. Gumball's hand felt cold and frail. 'Thank you for helping us get here,' Ulf said to him.

Tiana glowed furiously. 'But he stole it from you, Ulf!'

'We don't need it any more,' Ulf told her. 'Come on, it's time to save Dr Fielding and Orson.'

He stepped past the pedal-carts to the wooden door, then looked over his shoulder. 'Gumball, are you coming too?'

The little goblin was polishing the silver compass. 'No. I keep watch,' he muttered, stepping into the shadows.

'Oh, sure he will,' Tiana said, flying to Ulf's shoulder. 'He'll be off as soon as we're inside. He only came for your compass.'

The goblin's white eyes were blinking in the shadows. Ulf smiled, then he pushed the big wooden door open and stepped inside. He found himself in a stone corridor. Ulf glanced down a line of flaming torches lighting the walls. He could hear a voice coming from beyond a stone archway at the end of the corridor: 'AND THIS IS WHAT YOU'LL BE HUNTING!'

It was the voice of Baron Marackai…

CHAPTER FIFTEEN

Ulf crept along the flame-lit corridor past doors marked TROPHY PROCESSING ROOM, BAIT ROOM and ARMOURY. He stopped at the stone archway, hidden in the shadows. Tiana flew beside him and hovered above three levers sticking out from the wall.

They peered into what looked like dungeons. Standing less than ten metres away, with his back to them, was Baron Marackai. The Baron was dressed in a fur coat and serpent-skin boots. With him were five humans in camouflage clothing.

'Hunters,' Ulf whispered.

They were facing a row of cages. Inside

each cage a big green troll was snorting and grunting.

'As you can see,' Baron Marackai said, 'we have gathered only the finest specimens. Each of them is young and unblemished. Their heads will look splendid displayed on the walls of your homes.'

Baron Marackai led the hunters along the row of cages.

'Ven can ve kill zem?' a man with a red face asked.

'Not long now, Herr Pinkel. In just a few moments, I shall release these beasts into our magnificent hunting range where you can pursue them with weapons of your choice.'

'We no be in danger?' a man with a ponytail asked.

'Of course not, Señor Pedroso. I can assure you that these beasts do not stand a chance. Everything has been carefully designed to the hunter's advantage.'

At that moment, Ulf heard a clattering

sound from back down the corridor; a pedal-cart was pulling up in the tunnel.

'Quick, Ulf, hide,' Tiana whispered.

Ulf crawled quietly into the dungeons and hid behind a large wooden crate. It smelt of meat.

Tiana perched on his shoulder. They peered around the side of the crate as the Baron's men entered through the archway.

The Baron turned to the men. 'About time, too,' he said. 'Are the machines ready?'

'All oiled and greased, Sir,' Blud replied.

'Marvellous!'

The Baron faced the hunters. He smiled. 'Tonight marks our opening night, so I have prepared a special treat for you, a bonus prize for one lucky shooter.'

The Baron strode along the cages. At the end of the row was a cage draped in camouflage netting. He pulled the netting aside. 'Imagine that big head on your wall!'

The hunters gasped.

'A giant!' a big black man in sunglasses said.

'Not just any giant, Mr Biggles,' the Baron replied. 'This is the RSPCB's giant!'

Inside the cage, Ulf saw Orson lying on the floor unconscious.

Bone stepped across with a bucket of water and threw it over the giant.

Orson's eyes opened and he slowly sat up. 'What's going on?' he groaned.

'Welcome to Loadem Lodge,' the Baron said through the bars.

Orson stood up, hunched over. He was too big for the cage. He saw the trolls in the cages alongside him. 'What are they doing here?'

'The same as you, Mr Orson,' the Baron replied. 'Preparing to die.'

The hunters laughed.

A man in a cowboy hat pointed his finger like a gun. 'Pow! Pow! I'm gonna get that giant!'

'There's plenty of him to aim for, Mr Armstrong,' the Baron replied.

Orson shook the bars of his cage. 'Where's Dr Fielding?' he demanded.

Baron Marackai grinned. 'Oh, that reminds me. Blud, fetch the bait!'

Blud left the room, and a moment later Ulf heard an engine start. Blud rode back through the archway on a black motorbike, dragging Dr Fielding on a rope. She was being pulled along the stone floor.

'What has he done to her?' Tiana whispered in horror.

Dr Fielding's hands and feet were tied, her mouth was gagged with a crusty red rag and she was wrapped in a blanket of meaty steaks.

The trolls started grunting and drooling when they smelt the steaks. They clattered their tusks against the bars.

Baron Marackai was laughing. 'Oh, I do love your outfit, Dr Fielding,' he said, prodding one of the steaks with his finger.

'I'll crush you, Marackai,' Orson boomed from his cage.

The Baron turned. 'Empty threats in the circumstances, Mr Orson.'

He faced the hunters. 'Everyone, please do

show your appreciation for Dr Fielding, the RSPCB vet.'

'Boo! Hiss!' the hunters cried.

'Tonight, she will be our bait. We shall use her to lure the trolls to your guns.'

Dr Fielding lay wriggling on the floor, wrapped in the meat blanket and unable to stand.

The Baron raised his right hand. 'Death to the RSPCB!' he said.

The hunters held up their right hands and folded down their little fingers. 'Death to the RSPCB!'

Ulf clenched his fist.

'Ulf, don't do anything stupid,' Tiana warned.

'Hunters, it's time to begin the hunt!'

Ulf leapt over the crate. 'Stop!' he shouted, diving and knocking Baron Marackai to the floor.

'Werewolf!' the Baron cried. 'What are y—'

Ulf bashed him on the nose.

'Ouch! Bone, get him off me!'

Ulf felt a pair of strong hands dragging him

off. The big man threw Ulf to the floor, pinning him down with his boot.

'Well, well,' Baron Maracka said, standing up and rubbing his nose. 'So you decided to join us after all, werewolf.' He glanced to the hunters. 'I loathe werewolves,' he said.

A woman with a moustache peered down at Ulf. 'Can we hunt it?' she asked.

'Not this one, Lady Semolina,' Baron Maracka said. 'This beast's mine.'

Ulf was struggling beneath Bone's boot. It was pressed hard to his chest and he could barely breathe.

'Leave him alone or I'll tear your arms off!' Orson called through the bars of his cage.

Baron Maracka laughed. 'No you won't, Mr Orson. You're going in the Predatron where you'll be killed like any other beast. Hunters, fetch your weapons! BONE, BRING THE WEREWOLF TO THE PROCESSING ROOM!'

CHAPTER SIXTEEN

Ulf was carried, punching and struggling, down the stone corridor to a room that was writhing with rats.

'Lay him on the guillotine,' the Baron said.

Bone dumped Ulf on to a contraption in the middle of the room.

'Face up,' the Baron ordered.

Bone flipped Ulf on to his back, pressing him flat on a bench. Ulf scratched Bone's arm.

'Ow! Stop squirming, you little twerp.'

'Tie him,' Baron Marackai said. He stood at the end of the contraption and pulled on a rope.

The big man pushed Ulf's head out over

the end of the bench and began wrapping him in chains.

Ulf looked up.

As the Baron pulled the rope, a large metal blade was lifting high above Ulf's neck.

'You'll never get away with this,' Ulf said.

'Oh, but I will,' the Baron replied, grinning. 'The RSPCB is finished.'

Bone pulled the chains tight around Ulf's legs and arms. 'Can I do the chopping?' the big man asked.

'Not yet,' Baron Marackai said. 'I want his beast head.'

The blade was suspended above Ulf, ready to drop. The Baron tied the rope to a hook on the floor, then stepped to the wall and reached up, opening a high metal hatch. A cold wind blew in and Ulf could see the sky outside. Evening was setting in.

'The moon will rise soon,' the Baron told him, checking Ulf's chains. 'Wrap more on, Bone. I don't want him breaking free when he transforms.'

Bone wrapped more chains around Ulf and fastened their ends with a padlock. He took the key from the lock and handed it to the Baron.

'Splendid,' Baron Marackai said, slipping the key into the pocket of his fur coat.

Ulf tried to move his arms and legs, but he couldn't.

'There's no point struggling, werewolf,' the Baron said. 'You're not getting out alive.'

Ulf twisted his neck and saw a basket below his head at the end of the bench. It was writhing with rats.

The Baron felt in the basket and pulled out a chewed piece of meat. 'Come and finish your dinner, little rats,' he said. The Baron wiped the meat up and down the rope that secured the guillotine blade.

Ulf saw the rats scurry to the rope. They started chewing it.

'Enjoy your transformation, werewolf. It will be your last,' the Baron said. He rubbed the stump on his right hand where his little finger was missing. 'You've messed up my plans once

too often. But soon I'll be rid of you. Farraway Hall will be mine.'

'Farraway Hall belongs to the RSPCB,' Ulf said. 'Professor Farraway never wanted you to have it.'

The Baron stepped to the door. 'My father was a traitor to the Farraway name,' he spat. 'Come on, Bone. It's time to go hunting.'

Ulf looked up at the blade, then at the rats gnawing the rope. 'Let me out!' he shouted, struggling.

As the Baron and Bone left the room, the Baron glanced over his shoulder. 'Now, now, werewolf. Try not to lose your head.'

He grinned, then slammed the door shut behind him.

* * *

'Bone, start the machines!' the Baron ordered.

The big man headed off down the corridor to the pedal-carts.

Baron Marackai walked to the archway. He

stood by three levers on the wall, looking into the dungeons.

Blud was revving the engine on his motorbike. The trolls were oofing, reaching through the bars trying to grab Dr Fielding in the blanket of meat. The hunters were waiting with weapons: pistols and rifles, bows and arrows, knives and harpoon guns.

Chuck Armstrong was spinning a pistol on his finger. 'Let's get this party started,' he said.

'Gentlemen, Lady Semolina, if you would join me behind the security door?'

The hunters filed out into the corridor, and the Baron pulled a lever on the wall. Metal bars lowered in the archway, sealing off the dungeons. The hunters peered in through the bars.

'Blud, get ready with the bait!'

Blud revved his engine. He turned the bike to face the end wall of the dungeons, then the Baron pulled a second lever and the end wall started lifting up, revealing the snowy valley outside. It stretched out in front of the dungeons. The snow looked blood-red in the setting sun. Spotlights came on in the valley, lighting up machines and contraptions on either side.

'Behold the Predatron!' the Baron said. 'The most thrilling hunting range known to man.'

Blud sped out on the motorbike, dragging Dr Fielding along the snow wrapped in the blanket of meat.

Baron Marackai pulled a third lever and the doors of the cages sprang open. The trolls bounded out, charging on all fours into the Predatron, following the scent of the meat.

Orson glanced at the Baron. 'You'll pay for this,' he said.

'Hadn't you better save your precious Dr Fielding from those trolls?' the Baron chuckled. 'Run, Mr Orson, run!' The Baron grinned as Orson shook his fist, then strode out into the valley.

'Hunters, proceed to your vehicles!' Baron Marackai said. He turned and marched the hunters down the corridor and through the big wooden door.

Each hunter jumped into a pedal-cart, clutching their weapons.

'Let's hunt these beasts!' the Baron told them. As he stepped into a cart, the Baron felt a tug on his coat. He pulled it into the cart then sat down and pedalled off up the tunnel.

'Yee-ha!' Chuck Armstrong shouted, excitedly.

Lady Semolina blew loudly on a hunting horn.

The Baron rubbed his hands together.

'FIRST STOP: SKITTLE ALLEY!'

CHAPTER SEVENTEEN

Ulf lay beneath the guillotine struggling in the chains. He glanced up at the blade, then across to the rats chewing on the blood-stained rope. Through the open hatch, he could see the sky darkening. Any moment now the full moon would rise.

A trail of sparkles burst through the hatch. It was Tiana!

'Ulf!' she called. 'They've dragged Dr Fielding into the Predatron. They're hunting Orson and the trolls. We've got to do something!'

'I can't move,' Ulf called.

Tiana flew to the guillotine blade. 'Oh my goodness,' she said.

'Quick, stop the rats!' Ulf told her.

Tiana saw the rats gnawing the rope. She flew down and kicked one on the nose. The rat snapped at her tiny foot and she darted out of the way. Tiana grabbed the rat's tail and tugged it, trying to pull the rat from the rope, but the rat flicked its tail sideways, sending her hurtling across the room. Tiana picked herself up from the floor and flew back. Rats were scurrying up and down the rope, gnawing and chewing it. She blasted them with sparkles and they squeaked and scattered. Then they turned and ran back again. 'It's no use, Ulf,' Tiana said, pulling a rat's whiskers. 'I can't stop them!'

The rope was fraying where the rats were chewing it.

Ulf stared at the guillotine blade. 'You have to try,' he said. 'I can't get out.'

He wriggled in the chains, but they were fastened tight. 'I'm locked in,' he said, glancing at the padlock.

Tiana kicked and punched the rats. She blasted and prodded them, but they kept nibbling the rope. 'There are hundreds of them!' she screamed. The rope was creaking, about to snap.

Just then, the door opened. A head poked in with large white eyes, pointy ears and a fat snout.

'Gumball!' Ulf said.

It was the little goblin. He scampered in.

'Oh, that's all we need!' Tiana cried, tugging a rat's ear.

The goblin held out his bony hand. 'Shiny,' he said, smiling. He was holding the key to the padlock!

'Where did you get that?' Ulf asked.

'I took it from the nasty man,' Gumball said, proudly.

The blade was hanging by a single strand.

'Quickly!' Ulf said.

Gumball put the key in the padlock. 'Friend,' he said, turning it.

At that moment, a silvery light shone into the room. Ulf looked up at the open hatch. He could see the moon outside. His eyes flashed silver and he felt the bones in his chest cracking. His skeleton began realigning. Dark hair started growing over his whole body. A thick tail grew from the base of his spine. His nails lengthened into claws. His muscles bulged. Fangs split through his gums. He tore off the chains and sprang forwards just as a rat bit through the last strand of the rope. The guillotine blade slewed down the wooden uprights, thudding into the ground.

Ulf looked out at the moon and howled.

'Gumball, you did it!' Tiana called, flying to the goblin. 'You saved Ulf!'

She planted a kiss on Gumball's fat snout. 'Sorry I was mean to you,' she said.

Gumball blushed.

'The others need saving now,' Ulf growled. He leapt up and scrambled through the open hatch.

'Go, werewolf! Go!' the little goblin called.

Ulf bounded into the Predatron.

CHAPTER EIGHTEEN

In the moonlight, far up ahead, Ulf could see the trolls lumbering through the Predatron. Spotlights shone from the steep slopes on either side of the valley, their beams criss-crossing the snowy ground.

As a wolf, Ulf's senses were sharp. He could smell the trolls' fear. He could hear Baron Marackai's voice: 'Let the fun begin!'

Ulf bounded on all fours, following the meaty trail in the snow where Dr Fielding had been dragged behind the motorbike.

'Be careful, Ulf,' Tiana cried, flying after him.

Ulf scanned the valleysides. He saw Baron Marackai high up, standing by a hatch, holding a megaphone to his mouth. 'Bone, show us the beasts!'

On the side of the valley a spotlight swivelled, sweeping a beam of light on to the trolls. Ulf saw Orson striding after them.

'Release the boulders!' the Baron called. 'Knock them down like skittles!'

Ulf heard a clanking sound and the creaking of levers. He saw a large metal chute pointing down into the valley. It was moving, aiming for the trolls. With a loud rumble, a boulder rolled down the chute. It thundered into the valley and tore across the ground like a huge bowling ball, just missing the trolls.

'Bone! More boulders!' the Baron called.

The metal chute swung sideways, adjusting its aim. A second boulder rolled down and Ulf saw Orson run to protect the trolls. The giant stepped in front of them and smashed the boulder away with his fist. A third boulder came hurtling after. Orson caught it and threw it to the side of the valley. Then he blocked another with his shoulder. Boulder after

boulder came thundering down. Orson tried to block them, but there were too many for him to stop. One of them struck a troll, knocking it to the ground.

'Troll down!' Baron Marackai shouted. 'Guns at the ready!'

Ulf started running for the fallen troll, Tiana whizzing alongside him. He saw five hatches open in the valleyside. The five hunters appeared, each holding a gun. The spotlight shone on the troll.

'Fire!' Marackai commanded.

Shots echoed around the valley and bullets whizzed through the air.

'BANG GOES A TROLL!' the Baron called.

The hunters cheered.

Then the troll sat up, shaking its head.

'It's still alive! You missed!' Baron Marackai called. 'Reload, hunters!'

The hunters took aim at the troll as it was getting to its feet.

'Fire!'

As more shots rang out, Ulf saw Orson

throw himself in front of the troll. The bullets thudded into Orson's chest and he crashed to the ground.

'Bang goes the giant!' the Baron laughed.

'Yee-ha! I got him,' Ulf heard.

'Well done, Mr Armstrong,' the Baron called. 'Hunters, back into your carts. Next stop: the Drowning Pool!'

The hatches slammed shut and the spotlight swivelled, sweeping its beam up the valley.

Ulf raced to Orson. The giant was slumped on the ground. There were bullet holes in his shirt.

'He's dead, Ulf!' Tiana said.

Slowly, Orson sat up. He put his hand inside his shirt and picked out a bullet. He winked at Ulf and smiled. 'Good job I packed my chainmail vest,' he said.

Tiana hugged Orson's ear. 'Thank goodness you're okay.'

Ulf grinned with his fangs. Then he glanced up ahead. He could see the trolls further up the Predatron, sniffing the ground.

'Come on,' he said. 'They're in danger.'

CHAPTER NINETEEN

Ulf raced after the trolls. They were approaching a wide expanse of water that spanned the width of the valley. Ulf could see the meaty trail from Dr Fielding's blanket leading on to a rusty metal bridge.

'Dr Fielding went that way, Tiana,' he said, pointing over the water.

Ulf bounded ahead of the trolls and leapt on to the bridge. He looked down, seeing the full moon reflected below him. Then he felt the bridge wobble and looked back. The trolls were following behind him.

'Ulf, watch out!' Tiana screamed, flying overhead. She pointed across the water.

Standing on the far bank at the end of the bridge was Baron Marackai.

Ulf growled and ran for him.

'What are you doing here, werewolf? You're meant to be dead!' Baron Marackai said. He put the megaphone to his mouth. 'Hunters, we have a new beast in the Predatron. A pesky werewolf!'

The Baron pulled a long lever at the end of the bridge.

Ulf felt the bridge drop away beneath him. He grabbed for the handrail but grasped thin air. He splashed into the cold water below. He kicked his legs, and flicked his tail to swim. He could hear splashing and oofing. The trolls were in the water behind him, thrashing their arms.

'They're drowning!' Tiana cried, flying above them.

'Trolls down!' Ulf heard Baron Marackai call. His voice rang around the valley. 'And the werewolf!'

On the left-hand side of the valley, the hunters stepped out on to a metal balcony.

'Harpoons at the ready!' Baron Marackai called up.

The hunters each pointed a harpoon gun.

'Fire!'

Five metal harpoons whistled through the air and struck the water. A troll squealed.

'Good shot, Herr Pinkel!' the Baron called.

Ulf turned, swimming towards the troll. A harpoon was stuck in its arm. He pulled the harpoon out, then began dragging the troll through the water.

Baron Marackai was looking at Ulf from the shore. 'How dare you, werewolf!' he shouted. 'You're spoiling our fun!'

As Ulf started pushing the troll to the bank, the Baron climbed into a hatch in the ground and disappeared.

The troll slowly pulled itself up and Ulf climbed out after it.

Just then, he heard an almighty splash behind him. Ulf turned and saw Orson wading in the water. The giant was so tall he could stand. He was pushing the other four trolls, two with each arm, towards the shore. 'Stay there, Ulf,' Orson called. 'Help them out.'

Orson lifted a troll from the water and Ulf grabbed its arm.

'Reload and fire again!' he heard. He looked up to the valleyside and saw Baron Marackai appear on the balcony with the hunters.

'Aim for the giant!' the Baron ordered.

'Leave this to me,' Tiana said. She shot over the water and up the valleyside to Lady Semolina. She blew sparkles in the woman's face. Then she flew to Pedro Pedroso and kicked him on the nose. She punched Herman Pinkel in the eye. One by one, the five hunters retreated from the balcony, backing through a door in the side of the valley.

'Come back!' Baron Marackai called. 'It's only a fairy!'

Tiana flew down.

'Thanks, Tiana,' Orson said.

The trolls were lumbering away, sniffing the ground. They were safe – for now.

Baron Marackai clapped his hands. 'Oh, what a bunch of heroes you are,' he called. 'Well, let's see how you deal with the Forest of Fear.'

He left the balcony, disappearing into the valleyside.

Orson pulled himself out of the Drowning Pool and sat on the bank. He took off his boots and tipped them up. Icy water poured out. 'Bit nippy for a swim,' he said.

Ulf looked up the Predatron. The trolls were moving towards a silvery forest. 'Let's go!' he said, bounding after them.

Tiana raced alongside him. 'Hurry up, Orson,' she called.

The giant was pulling his boots on, hobbling behind. 'I'm coming as fast as I can.'

CHAPTER TWENTY

The Forest of Fear was made of metal. Ulf padded between tall trees of twisted iron, their spiked branches blocking out the moonlight. He ducked under rusting leaves and crept past bushes of barbed wire, peering into the shadows. He could hear the trolls snuffling up ahead, following the scent of the meat.

'Be careful,' Orson whispered, pushing through the metal branches.

'It's creepy in here,' Tiana said. 'I don't like it.'

Ulf moved stealthily, his paws scrunching in the snow. Suddenly, he heard a twanging sound and an arrow whizzed through the branches. 'Hunters,' he said, crouching low.

‘Where are they?’ Tiana asked, darting behind a rusty leaf. ‘I can’t see them.’

Another arrow whistled through the trees. The trolls roared and Ulf heard them clattering through the metal undergrowth, scattering in all directions.

Orson strode off. ‘Keep with them,’ he said, pushing through the forest, snapping the iron branches with his bare hands.

To his left, Ulf heard a loud squeal and a crash of metal. He rushed towards the sound and saw a big net swinging from a tree. A troll was trapped in it.

A hatch sprang open by a bush and Biggy popped up, aiming a longbow and arrow. He fired at the troll and the beast roared.

Ulf leapt for the hunter.

‘Holy hotdogs!’ Biggy cried, seeing Ulf coming for him.

Biggy ducked back underground, slamming the metal hatch behind him. Ulf landed with a thud on top of the hatch and tried to prise it open. It was stuck. He could hear a bolt

being drawn underground then the squeaking pedals of a cart trundling away beneath the forest floor.

'Up here, Ulf!' Tiana called. She was circling the troll in the net.

Ulf leapt up and slashed the net with his claws, cutting the troll free. It landed with a thud in the snow then stood up, staring at Ulf with wide eyes. It was a young male and looked frightened.

'Do not fear me,' Ulf growled. He gently bit the arrow in the troll's leg and pulled it out with his teeth. The troll grunted then lumbered away through the forest, sniffing the snow.

Ulf heard the Baron's voice again, calling: 'Get the werewolf!'

A hatch opened in the metal trunk of a tree. Pedro Pedroso popped out, aiming a crossbow. He fired at Ulf. Ulf dodged and an arrow shot past him, just clipping his bushy tail. The hatch in the tree slammed shut and Ulf heard the hunter climbing down a metal ladder underground. Ulf bounded away on all fours.

'Watch out!' Tiana called, flying after him.

The sharp point of another arrow flashed in the moonlight. Ulf ducked and it ricocheted off a metal branch. Then a knife flew past, spinning through the air. It landed in a barbed-wire bush. Ulf kept low as he raced through the trees, until finally he saw moonlight ahead.

He found Orson at the edge of the forest, trying to calm a troll. The giant was pulling netting from its tusks.

'Easy there, girl. We'll get you out of here,' the giant said. The troll grunted as Orson let it go. It lumbered out of the forest, following Dr Fielding's scent.

'Orson, are they all okay?' Tiana asked.

'They all made it,' the giant said.

Below ground, Ulf could hear pedal-carts squeaking. The hunters were moving up the Predatron. 'It's not over yet,' he warned.

CHAPTER TWENTY-ONE

Ulf sprinted ahead of Orson and Tiana, trying to catch up with the trolls.

The valley narrowed to a thin passageway between sheer metal walls over thirty metres high. It was illuminated by a string of electric light bulbs. The trolls were funnelling into it, sniffing in a line. Ulf ran in after them.

'Bone, start the Crusher!' he heard. Baron Marackai was standing at the very top of the right-hand wall, peering down.

From behind the metal walls came the rumbling sounds of engines. Clumps of snow began falling into the valley as the walls started moving inwards. Up ahead, the trolls began roaring. The passageway was narrowing. The trolls started oofing, beating their fists against the walls. The Crusher was trapping them.

'Hunters, load your weapons!' Baron Marackai called.

Ulf looked up and saw five guns pointing down.

'Take aim! F—'

Suddenly, there was a loud clang and the wrenching sound of straining metal pistons.

'Blud! Bone! What's happening?' Baron Marackai called.

Something was wrong with the Crusher.

Ulf looked back. Orson was at the entrance, pulling the metal walls apart with his mighty hands. Tiana was hovering above him. 'Heave, Orson! Heave!' she cried.

Ulf could hear the engines grinding. There was a sputtering sound then a loud bang as the Crusher broke and the lights went out. The walls started edging apart.

'Quick, fire at will!' the Baron called.

The hunters' guns blasted, but as the trolls

ran out, the bullets missed, sparking on the metal walls.

Orson came striding towards Ulf. 'Nothing's stronger than a giant,' he said.

Ulf looked up. He saw Baron Marackai silhouetted against the full moon. The Baron was shaking his fist. 'You and your miserable friends, werewolf! I'll get you!' he spat. 'It's time for war!'

The Baron fired an orange flare into the sky. It hung in the air, lighting the valley ahead. Ulf hurried out of the Crusher and in the orange light he could see the trolls sniffing through a wide section of the Predatron, following the meaty trail in the snow.

The Baron appeared on a balcony at the side of the valley and raised his megaphone. 'Let battle commence!'

Five hatches opened in the valleyside and the hunters threw hand grenades down. The grenades blasted huge craters in the snow.

The trolls started stampeding. A metal disc sprang up from the ground, tossing a troll into the air. Ulf heard the whizz of bullets, then a thud as the troll landed. It stood up, its legs wobbling.

'Missed!' Baron Marackai called. 'Can't you hit a moving target? Bone, fix the trolls to the spot! Start the Sticky Stucky!'

A large tube poked out from the hillside. It blasted a volley of black balls. They burst as they landed, splattering pools of glue on the ground. A troll ran into the glue. Its feet stuck and it roared with rage as it tried to move.

'That's it,' the Baron called. 'Now roll the logs, Blud!'

Tree trunks began tumbling down the valleyside. They knocked a troll to the ground.

'Now turn on the gas!' Baron Marackai called.

Ulf heard a hissing sound and columns of yellow gas shot up from pipes in the ground. The gas drifted across the valley, stinging Ulf's eyes. Ahead he could make out a troll crawling from the gas, tears streaming down its face.

'Boo hoo hooo,' Baron Marackai called. 'Start the Demolition Ball!'

There was a loud cranking sound. In the centre of the valley Ulf saw the tall pole with the huge metal ball attached by a chain. The pole began turning. The metal ball began swinging on its chain. It swung in circles, skimming the snow, faster and faster. The metal ball struck a troll and sent it flying.

'Start the Claw!' Baron Maracκai called.

At the side of the valley Ulf saw the crane with the mechanical claw. Its long metal arm was moving, lowering the claw to the ground. The claw closed around the troll's leg, then lifted it up and dangled it above the valley.

A second orange flare went off in the sky. The trolls were roaring: stuck in glue, choking on gas, springing through the air and dazed from the Demolition Ball and rolling logs.

'Hunters, kill at will!' the Baron called.

'Ulf, we've got to save them!' Tiana cried.

Ulf snarled. 'It's time to hunt the hunters!'

CHAPTER TWENTY-TWO

Ulf scanned the valley, locating the hunters. He saw Pedro Pedroso at a hatch high up in the side of the valley. Ulf bounded across the snow on all fours. He leapt on to a metal disc and a spring pinged him towards the valleyside. He struck the metal wall, gripping with his claws. Above him, he saw Pedro Pedroso loading a rifle. Ulf climbed up to the hatch and lunged for the gun, biting it in half with his teeth.

The hunter screamed. 'Ay Carumba!'

Ulf reached into the hatch and pulled Pedro Pedroso out by his ponytail. Pedro Pedroso tumbled head over heels down the valleyside and into the snow. He landed in a pool of glue. He tried to get up but he was stuck. 'Ayuda! Sticky stucky!' he shouted.

Tiana flew over to the hunter and blasted him with her sparkles. 'Go, Ulf!' she called.

Ulf pulled himself through the hatch. Now he was back inside the workings of the Predatron. He dropped on to the metal tracks and followed them along the tunnel. Ahead, he could see a pedal-cart parked and Herman Pinkel leaning out through a hatch. Ulf crept up quietly behind the hunter and snarled.

Herman Pinkel turned. 'Achtung Volf!' the hunter cried, dropping his rifle. He stepped back, his legs trembling, and fell on to a stack of tree trunks at the side of the tunnel.

'Fun's over,' Ulf growled. He pulled a lever and the wall of the tunnel swung open. The tree trunks thundered out, taking Herman Pinkel with them.

'Ouch! Oo! Argh!' the hunter cried, as he tumbled down into the valley.

Ulf licked his fangs.

'Over here, Ulf,' Tiana called, hovering above a hatch that was opening in the snowy ground. Chuck Armstrong popped up from the hatch, spinning two pistols on his fingers. He pointed them at a troll as it lumbered through the yellow gas.

Ulf turned and bounded along the track inside the Predatron. He saw a sign marked **GAS ATTACK** and raced steeply downwards under the valley. In a tunnel ahead of him, he saw Chuck Armstrong's legs. The hunter was standing at the top of a ladder.

He heard the hunter shooting. Ulf dived to a gas pipe at the base of the ladder and bit it in two. A jet of yellow gas shot up, blasting Chuck Armstrong out through the hatch. Ulf scrambled up the ladder and saw the hunter crawling in the snow surrounded by gas.

He was crying like a baby. 'I want my mummy.'

Ulf saw the troll lumbering away. Chuck Armstrong had missed.

He looked for Tiana and saw a flash of

flames burst in the distance. Up the valley Biggy was holding a flame-thrower, running towards a troll. It had been hit by the Demolition Ball and was stumbling, dazed.

Suddenly, Biggy stopped. A sparkle was darting around his head. Ulf smiled. Tiana was attacking the hunter. Flames shot high into the air as the big man staggered in the snow, trying to blast the fairy with his flame-thrower. Tiana swooped and dodged.

'Go, Tiana!' Ulf called.

The Demolition Ball was circling. Orson strode over and grabbed hold of it. He swung the ball towards Biggy.

Tiana zoomed away and the Demolition Ball smashed into the big man.

'Aaghhhhhhhh!' Biggy called, hurtling across the valley.

Ulf heard Baron Marackai's voice from the valleyside: 'You wretched, horrible, meddling beasts!'

The Baron was spitting with fury. 'Shoot them all, Lady Semolina!'

Lady Semolina was on a balcony swivelling a machine gun into position.

'No you don't,' Ulf growled. He raced across the valley towards the Claw. He leapt into the control cabin, and pulled a lever. The crane arm extended. He pulled another and the arm swung above the balcony. He pulled a third and the metal claw opened.

As Lady Semolina started firing, Ulf lowered the metal claw on to her, closing it around her waist. He lifted her off the bridge and swung her over the valley.

'Help me!' she cried, her legs jiggling in the air.

Ulf sprang from the crane and snarled.

'Nice work, Ulf,' Orson called. The giant came striding to Ulf's side. Tiana came flying after.

'That showed those hunters,' the fairy said.

'You haven't won yet!' the Baron shouted. He was pointing to the far end of the valley. 'Aren't you forgetting dear Dr Fielding?'

The five trolls were up ahead, following

the meaty trail through the snow. They were heading towards a big metal archway with coloured lights flashing around its edge. The lights spelt out the words **FEEDING TROUGH**.

'IT'S TIME FOR THE TROLLS' SUPPER!' the Baron called.

CHAPTER TWENTY-THREE

'You save Dr Fielding,' Orson said to Ulf. 'Leave the trolls to me.'

Ulf bounded past the trolls and headed through the metal archway into a tall tunnel. He glanced back. Orson was blocking the entrance, stopping the trolls coming in. The giant's chainmail vest rattled as the trolls butted and charged him. 'Now there's no need for that,' Orson said.

Tiana flew among the trolls, shining her light in their eyes. 'You're not allowed in there.'

'Good thinking, Tiana,' Orson said. 'Keep them back.'

Ulf sprinted through the tunnel and out the

other side into a round snowy expanse with sheer metal walls. He saw balconies, and a ring of floodlights lighting up the snow. In the centre of the valley, a large metal feeding trough lay on the ground. Beyond it were the entrances to dark tunnels. He looked up. He was facing Honeycomb Mountain. Its silhouette loomed over the end of the valley a hundred metres high.

Ulf saw something move in the feeding trough. Lying there, wrapped in the blanket of meat, was Dr Fielding. She was gagged and struggling, tied up in ropes and chains. He ran towards her.

'Going somewhere, werewolf?' he heard.

Ulf looked up. Baron Marackai was standing on a balcony, holding his megaphone to his mouth.

Ulf snarled.

'You're going the wrong way,' the Baron called. 'It's Mr Orson who's going to die first. Blud! Bone! Bury the giant!'

Ulf glanced back at the archway. Shards of

metal flew across the valley as it exploded in a flash of bright flames. A shockwave punched Ulf's chest, knocking him to the ground. He watched in horror as a cloud of smoke rose into the air, revealing a massive mound of snow and twisted iron. The archway had collapsed. Orson was buried beneath it.

'Orson!' Ulf cried, scrambling to his feet. He raced back and began digging frantically, pulling out twisted iron girders and throwing them aside.

Tiana flew up from behind the mound. 'Orson!' she was calling.

Ulf heaved aside a girder and saw the tip of Orson's finger poking out from underneath. He cleared the metal and snow from around the giant's hand. 'Orson, get up!' he called.

The hand lay heavy and still.

Tiana perched on Orson's fingertip. 'No!' she cried. 'Poor Orson.' A tear rolled down her cheek.

Ulf looked up. He could hear the trolls clambering up the far side of the mound, sniffing and grunting. They were coming for their dinner.

'Save Dr Fielding…!' Tiana cried.

There was nothing Ulf could do for Orson now. He turned back and ran towards the Feeding Trough.

From the balcony, the Baron called through his megaphone: 'Blud! Bone! Stop the werewolf!'

Below the Baron, a metal door opened and Blud and Bone stepped out on to the snow. The big man was holding an iron bar, and the small man was cowering behind him.

'You get him, Bone,' Blud said.

Ulf snarled as the big man came running towards him.

Bone swung the iron bar.

Ulf dodged, and the bar whipped past his ear, just clipping his fur.

Blud kept hidden behind Bone. 'That's it, sock it to him,' the small man said.

Bone swung the iron bar again.

Ulf dived to the side, landing in the snow.

The big man stood over him, clutching the iron bar in both hands.

'Now you've got him. Knock him out,' Blud said, peeking from between Bone's legs.

As the iron bar came thumping down into the snow, Ulf rolled. He leapt up, grabbed the bar in his jaws and bit it in two.

'Bloomin' heck,' Bone said, stepping back.

Ulf snarled at the big man, showing his fangs.

'Now what do I do, Blud?' Bone asked.

'Run!' Blud yelled.

Both men started running back to the door in the valleyside.

'Come back, you pathetic cowards!' Baron Marackai cried.

Blud and Bone raced through the door, slamming it shut behind them.

'I'll deal with you myself, werewolf!' the Baron called.

Ulf glanced across and saw the Baron jumping off the balcony into the snow. Then he heard trolls grunting. He glanced back at the fallen archway. The trolls had climbed over the mound and were heading for the Feeding Trough. Ulf leapt to Dr Fielding. He bit through the chains and ropes around her, then ripped off the blanket of meat.

She pulled off her gag. 'Thank you, Ulf!' she gasped, climbing out of the Feeding Trough.

'No you don't, werewolf!' Ulf heard.

On the far side of the trough, a hatch opened in the ground. Baron Maracka stepped out, pointing a pistol at Ulf. 'Now *you* can die!' he said.

As the Baron pulled the trigger, Ulf dived for cover into the Feeding Trough. The bullet ricocheted off the metal.

'Leave him alone!' Dr Fielding cried.

'Oh, okay, if you insist,' the Baron said. 'I shall leave him to the trolls instead.' The Baron started laughing. 'HA HA HAAA HAA HAAAAAAA HAAAAAAAAAAAAAA!'

Ulf peered out of the trough.

All five trolls were thundering towards him, slobbering. Ulf was lying with the meaty steaks!

Ulf leapt up and threw the blanket of meat over Baron Marackai. It landed on the Baron's head, covering him completely. Dr Fielding stepped forwards holding a chain, and looped it over the Baron's shoulders. She pulled it tight. The Baron struggled, hopping up and down, trying to wriggle out of the blanket of meat. 'Nooooooo!' he cried.

He started running away as the hungry trolls thundered past the Feeding Trough, chasing him.

Ulf and Dr Fielding watched as the Baron ran towards Honeycomb Mountain, the blanket of meat over his head. He smacked into the base of the mountain and fell backwards. Then he got up, his legs wobbling. He was feeling his way along the wall.

The trolls were charging on all fours towards him, gouging the air with their tusks.

The Baron reached a tunnel and ran inside. The trolls ran in after him. Ulf could hear their hungry grunts echoing as the Baron screamed: 'I'll be baaaaaack!'

Ulf watched, panting.

'Where's Orson?' Dr Fielding asked.

Ulf looked back at the mound of metal and snow where the archway had fallen. He could see Tiana's light glowing above Orson's finger. 'I couldn't save him,' Ulf replied.

As he stared at the mound, Ulf heard a rumble. The snow and metal started moving.

Orson was rising from beneath it.

Tiana flew up, sparkling. 'Orson's alive!' she called.

The giant rubbed his head and looked around. 'Has anyone seen those trolls?' he asked.

Ulf smiled, his fangs glinting. He looked up at the moon and howled.

CHAPTER TWENTY-FOUR

The next day, Ulf woke late with the sun on his face. He opened his eyes. He was back in his den at Farraway Hall. Folded outside his door were a pair of jeans and a T-shirt. He pulled them on and stepped out into the sunshine.

Tiana came flying from the paddock. 'Good afternoon, Ulf,' she said. 'You were brilliant last night!'

Ulf rubbed his eyes. 'Was I?' he asked.

'Don't you remember? You stopped the troll hunt. You saved Dr Fielding.'

Ulf licked his teeth. His fangs had receded back into his gums. The memory of his transformation was a blur.

'How did we get home?' he asked.

'Orson straightened the helicopter blades and we flew back this morning. After waiting for you, of course. You went wild last night, chasing snow hares. Dr Fielding let you loose in the mountains.'

Ulf smiled.

'Come on. Dr Fielding asked me to come and get you,' Tiana said.

The fairy flew off and Ulf followed her up the side of the paddock into the yard.

'Afternoon, Ulf,' he heard.

Orson came out of the feedstore. The giant had a crutch under his arm made from a tree trunk, and a bandage wrapped around his head.

'Are you okay, Orson?' Ulf asked.

'Nothing that a barrel of apples and a bucket of tea won't mend. You were brave last night, Ulf. You showed those hunters.'

'They'll all be behind bars by now,' Dr Fielding said, stepping out from the side-door of Farraway Hall. 'The department for

National and International Criminal Emergencies were very interested to hear what they'd been up to.'

'NICE?' Ulf said.

'I called NICE from Loadem Lodge. They've arrested the hunters and are dismantling the Predatron.'

Dr Fielding was carrying the bat-cage with Gumball's messenger bat inside. She smiled at Ulf. 'Thank you for saving me last night,' she said. She put the bat-cage down and gave Ulf a big hug.

'That's okay, Dr Fielding,' Ulf said, wriggling away.

He looked at the bat. It was nibbling a grasshopper, feeding up for its journey home. 'I couldn't have done it without Gumball. Gumball rescued me.'

'It seems Professor Farraway knew what he was doing, making Gumball a spotter,' Dr Fielding said. She glanced at Tiana and winked.

'I still think he smells.' Tiana giggled.

Dr Fielding knelt down and opened the door of the bat-cage. 'Would you like to release the messenger bat, Ulf?' she asked.

Ulf reached in and picked up Gumball's bat.

'One moment, Ulf,' Dr Fielding said. From the pocket of her white coat she took out a scrap of paper. On it, she'd written, *Thank You.*

Dr Fielding slipped the message into the ring on the bat's leg then Ulf released it into the air. He watched as it circled high above the yard then flew off over Farraway Hall.

'Bye bye, batty!' Ulf heard. Druce the gargoyle was bounding along the rooftop, waving.

Ulf watched the bat fly away until it was a tiny dot in the distance. 'What about the trolls?' he asked Dr Fielding.

'Trolls are tough beasts. They'll be fine,' she told him. 'Those young ones will be safely back with their families by now.'

Ulf wondered if they'd eaten the Baron.

'There's something I don't quite understand,' he said. 'How did Marackai know about the Predatron?'

Dr Fielding glanced at Orson. Orson nodded. 'I think there's something you should see, Ulf,' she said.

Ulf followed Dr Fielding into her office.

'You'd better sit down, Ulf. I'm afraid this is quite shocking.' On Dr Fielding's desk was a leatherbound photograph album. 'We found this at Loadem Lodge.'

Ulf sat in the chair at Dr Fielding's desk. He opened the album and started turning the pages. Ulf saw old black-and-white photographs. 'This is horrible,' he said.

In each photograph, a hunter was holding up the head of a dead beast mounted on a plaque like a trophy. There were troll heads… griffin heads… giranha heads… jackalope heads… and in one of the pictures a hunter was holding the head of a werewolf.

Ulf felt sick. 'How can humans be so cruel?' he asked.

'Those hunters aren't just any humans, Ulf. They're all Farraways,' Dr Fielding said. 'They're the Professor's ancestors.'

'Professor Farraway?' Ulf asked.

'The Professor was born into a long line of hunters, Ulf.'

'I don't understand,' Ulf said. 'The Professor was a good man.'

Dr Fielding turned the pages in the album to a photograph of a man standing beside a single metal tree. 'This man is the Professor's great-great-grandfather,' she said. 'It seems he built the Predatron.'

The man's face looked twisted and mean.

'Professor Farraway wasn't like the rest of his family, Ulf. He stopped the Predatron when he inherited the Farraway estate. He set up the RSPCB to protect beasts and to make amends for what his ancestors had done.'

Ulf felt shocked. 'You mean all the Farraways were bad?'

Then he remembered being chained to the guillotine. Marackai had called the Professor a traitor to the Farraway name.

'It wasn't Marackai who was the disgrace to the Farraway family, Ulf. It was the Professor.'

Dr Fielding closed the photograph album. 'It's over now, though,' she said. 'Marackai's gone, thanks to you.'

Dr Fielding whistled and the Helping Hand scuttled in. 'File this under Historical Hunting, will you please?'

The Helping Hand took the photograph album and carried it to a cupboard at the back of the room.

Dr Fielding opened her office door and Ulf followed her into the corridor. 'You should do something fun today, Ulf. You've had a tough night.'

'I'm okay,' Ulf said.

She ruffled his hair. 'Why don't you come to the hatching bay with me? We've got some jellystoats that are due to be born any moment.'

'I will in a bit,' Ulf told her. 'There's something I need to do first.'

Dr Fielding headed down the corridor. 'Okay, I'll see you later.'

Ulf ran up the back stairs. He raced through the Room of Curiosities and opened the library door. It was dark inside. 'Professor, are you in here?' he asked.

On a table by the end wall, a candle flickered on, lighting up a portrait of Professor Farraway.

'I know about your family,' Ulf said.

He stared at the painting, looking at the Professor's kind eyes. 'I've come to tell you that the Predatron's being dismantled,' he said. 'Marackai's gone.'

But as Ulf spoke, he felt an icy chill pass through him. The candle rose into the air.

'It's okay, Professor. It's over.'

The candle was drifting to the window. Ulf saw the corner of the curtain peeling back, revealing daylight and the beast park outside.

'We're safe, Professor,' he said. Then the hairs on Ulf's neck stood on end as an invisible finger began writing on the dusty glass: *BE ON YOUR GUARD. NO BEAST IS SAFE FROM HIM*

THE END ... FOR NOW

Now go online to
WWW.BEASTLYBUSINESS.COM
for free goodies and to join the RSPCB.

Have you read Ulf's other adventures in the *An Awfully Beastly Business* series?

Werewolf versus Dragon

Sea Monsters and other Delicacies

Keep a look out for Ulf's
next exciting adventure with

The Jungle Vampire